CAMBRIDGE PRIMARY
English

Learner's Book

5

Sally Burt and Debbie Ridgard

CAMBRIDGE
UNIVERSITY PRESS

CAMBRIDGE
UNIVERSITY PRESS

University Printing House, Cambridge CB2 8BS, United Kingdom

One Liberty Plaza, 20th Floor, New York, NY 10006, USA

477 Williamstown Road, Port Melbourne, VIC 3207, Australia

4843/24, 2nd Floor, Ansari Road, Daryaganj, Delhi – 110002, India

79 Anson Road, #06–04/06, Singapore 079906

Cambridge University Press is part of the University of Cambridge.

It furthers the University's mission by disseminating knowledge in the pursuit of education, learning and research at the highest international levels of excellence.

www.cambridge.org
Information on this title: www.cambridge.org/9781107683211

First published 2015
20 19 18 17

Printed in Dubai by Oriental Press

A catalogue record for this publication is available from the British Library

ISBN 978-1-107-68321-1 Paperback

Contents

Welcome to the *Cambridge Primary English* Series, Stage 5.

This Learner's Book takes you through Stage 5 of the Cambridge Primary curriculum. It contains nine units of lessons and activities to help you improve your reading, writing, speaking and listening skills. This book covers all the skills you need to develop in Stage 5.

Each term has two long units and one shorter one. Three units focus on fiction, three on non-fiction and three on poetry and plays. Each unit has a theme covering all sort of interesting topics. We hope you enjoy the variety and learn more about language and the different ways we express ourselves for different purposes.

These icons will show you how you're going to work:

have a discussion

do some reading

do some writing

role play, read out loud or do an oral activity

AZ do a spelling activity

Sometimes, your teacher will lead a discussion or explain an activity; sometimes you'll work in small groups or with a talk partner. At other times, you'll work alone. Some activities need you to read carefully to find specific information or notice particular techniques of writing, while other activities ask you to respond, discuss and even perform – especially the narrative poetry. All the activities have been designed to guide you and challenge you in your language adventure.

You'll find some extra help along the way, so look out for these features:

I am here to give you reminders and plenty of ideas.

Tip
These tips give you handy hints as you work.

Did you know?
These boxes encourage you to think broadly and do further research.

How did I do?
These boxes ask you to evaluate how you are doing. Answer the questions honestly – there is no right or wrong answer.

Language focus
These boxes explain helpful language rules. You'll need to remember the information to use again.

This course gives you the chance to share your ideas and check your progress and to build your confidence in expressing your own opinions orally or in your notebook.

On pages 143 to 148 you'll find helpful spelling rules and activities to practise and expand your knowledge of words and their spelling. You can go there whenever you like to check your own spelling skills.

On pages 149 to 158 you'll find a Toolkit – a set of resources you can use at any time. These include tools and tips such as an editing checklist, poetic devices and tips for making a speech.

We hope you enjoy the course and that it helps you to feel confident about responding to English, and using English in a variety of ways.

1 There's a lesson in that

Sometimes we can learn from stories as well as enjoy them. In this unit, you'll read fables – stories that were written to teach us a lesson. You'll practise writing in different styles and tell a fable of your own.

Vocabulary to learn and use: fable, moral, proverb, stereotype, idiom/idiomatic expression, figurative expression, human characteristics

1 Read a story by Aesop

A *The Ant and the Grasshopper* is one of Aesop's most famous fables.

1 Skim the story silently to get the main idea.
2 Read the story aloud in your group, one paragraph each.
  a Do you understand all the words in your paragraph?
  b Use expression as you read, so you make the meaning clear.

Did you know?

The storyteller Aesop is said to have lived in Greece in the 6th century BCE. No-one is sure where he came from but the name 'Aesop' comes from the Greek word 'Aethiop' meaning Ethiopia.

Tip

When you don't know what a word means, try these ideas:

• Break the word into syllables and look for a common root word, prefix or suffix.

• Re-read the word in context for extra clues.

• Use a dictionary.

The Ant and the Grasshopper

One fine summer's day, deep in a meadow, a grasshopper was bouncing about, chirruping and singing without a care in the world. An ant bustled by, weighed down by the enormous ear of corn she was lugging to her nest. Time and time again, the grasshopper watched the ant scurry back and forth gathering food – insects, flies, grains of wheat – anything she could find, never once stopping to admire the glorious day or relax in the rays.

The grasshopper found this difficult to **fathom** and teased her as she busied by, saying, "Take it easy there, Ant! I don't understand why you're working so hard. The day is long! Food is plentiful. Come and rest awhile, and listen to my latest melody."

"As it happens, Grasshopper, I am storing up food for winter and you should be doing the same. Summer won't last forever, you know," snapped the ant as she continued on her industrious way, if anything toiling just a little harder. The grasshopper **guffawed** at the idea of working on such a day and hopped happily off into the sunset, singing and jigging all the way.

And summer *didn't* last. It never does. Winter came, bringing barren fare and frosty fields. Grasshopper's song stuck in his throat as he shivered without shelter or sustenance, gazing wistfully at the ants as they munched liberally from their stores of food, shaking their heads at him and offering him nothing.

"How foolish I have been!" he wailed, for only then did Grasshopper understand that he should have made provision for winter as Ant had said.

Sally Burt

Who would you rather be friends with – Ant or Grasshopper?

guffaw *v.* to laugh loudly, especially to mock something

B 💬 **Discuss the story in a group.**

1 Can you summarise the main idea of the story in one sentence?
2 Who are the main characters? How are they different from each other in what they say and do?
3 One character learned something important. What was it?
4 Which character do you think behaved the best? Use examples to explain your view.

C ✏️ **Fables are found in many cultures and folklore storytelling traditions.**

1 What have you learned about fables from the story?
Write a Fable fact file in your notebook.

Fable fact file:
- Fables are …
- The characters are usually …
- The main point …
- We can …

Use these key words to help you:

short   moral   human characteristics   lesson   story

2 Discuss other stories you think might be fables.

How did I do?

- Did I understand the key features of a fable?
- Did I recognise whether a story is a fable from my notes?

D ✏️ **Complete your reading log for *The Ant and the Grasshopper*.**
Do you think a story is a good way of teaching this lesson?
Explain your opinion.

2 Check your understanding

(A) 🗩 🖹 **Discuss the questions with a talk partner and then write your answers neatly in your notebook. Use examples from the text.**

1 Why did Grasshopper tease Ant?
2 Why did Ant say "*summer won't last forever*"?
3 Give an example of Ant's **actions** to show she approves or disapproves of Grasshopper.
4 What made Grasshopper finally understand that he should have acted differently?
5 How do you think Ant felt when she saw Grasshopper at the end?

(B) 🖹 👥 **Verbs can tell you about characters through how they act and move.**

1 What different kinds of walking do these words describe? Role play them with a partner.

> stroll   amble   meander   stride   saunter   promenade   hike   pace

2 Choose a verb from the story that shows Ant's mood when Grasshopper teases her.
3 Write down verbs from the story to describe how Ant moves. What do they show about her personality?
4 *Fathom* has more than one meaning in the dictionary. Use the context to decide which meaning is correct in the story.
5 What tense is the narrative part of the story? Give three examples.
6 What tense is the dialogue mainly in? Give three examples.

(C) 🗩 🖹 **Punctuation is necessary in any story.**

1 Where are exclamation marks used and why?
2 Find an example of punctuation that shows where there is dialogue in the story.
3 Explain the reason for the apostrophe in each example:
   a *One fine summer's day ...*
   b *Summer won't last forever ...*
   c *And summer didn't last ...*
   d *The grasshopper's song stuck in his throat ...*

> **fathom**
> – *n.* a unit of measurement (equal to six feet) for water depth
> – *v.* to measure the depth of water with a sounding line
> – *v.* to understand something by thinking about it hard

3 Story features

Did you know?

A 🗨️📝 Animal characters in fables often have particular human characteristics that we associate with each animal. These are known as stereotypes.

> **Anthropomorphism** means giving human characteristics to animals in stories or pictures. *Anthropos* means 'man' or 'human' in Ancient Greek and *morph* means shape or form. Can you see how this word came about?

1 Discuss with a talk partner the characteristics often associated with these animals in stories.

elephant	fox	snake	lion

hyena	donkey	wolf	rabbit

2 How does Ant act like a person? Make a list.
3 How does Grasshopper act like a person? Make a list.
4 Write two short paragraphs describing the personalities of Ant and Grasshopper, using examples from the text of how they speak and act.
5 Read these fact files about real ants and grasshoppers.
   a Which is which?
   b Do the facts support Ant's and Grasshopper's personalities?

> I love having fun swimming and flapping about but I always remember that I need to find my own food!

A	B
• Live almost anywhere except extremely cold places	• Live almost anywhere
• Live by themselves	• Live in colonies
• Mostly eat grasses, leaves and cereal crops (herbivore)	• Will eat most things especially insects, meat, fats and sugary foods (omnivore)
• Don't usually survive the winter	• Can live a few months to a few years

B 💬 Stories usually contain an issue or a complication. In fables, the issue is the lesson learned by one of the characters.

1 Discuss the issue in this story.
2 What did either of the main characters do to resolve the problem?
3 How does the story teach us the lesson?

C 📝💬👥 Ant and Grasshopper approach life differently.

1 Make notes about how each character approaches life.
2 Summarise your ideas to your talk partner and discuss whether you agree.
3 Sort these adjectives into two lists to describe Ant and Grasshopper.

> practical   thoughtless   hard-working   optimistic   dull   happy-go-lucky
> fun-loving   chirpy   sensible   prudent   irresponsible   cheerful
> bossy   cheery   serious   worthy   unkind   down-to-earth   feckless

4 Role play a conversation in which Grasshopper asks Ant for help at the end of the story.
  a What will Grasshopper say?
  b How will Ant react?
  c What could Grasshopper offer Ant in exchange for food?
5 Write a short paragraph explaining what you would say and do if Grasshopper asked you for help. Give reasons.

4 What about my point-of-view?

A 💬📝 The narrator of a story can either be a character (first person) or someone looking in from outside (third person).

1 Who tells the story of *The Ant and the Grasshopper*?
2 What evidence tells you this – the narrative or the dialogue? Why?
3 Which words show whether these sentences are in first or third person?
  a Grasshopper said he hoped winter would not come.
  b I am worried that Grasshopper will have no food.
  c She works so hard and never has time for play.
  d We share all the food we collected to see us through winter.
  e The ants know they need to store food to survive.

Language focus

Third person narrative: an outsider tells the story but is not part of it.

Imran went to school early so that **he** could hand in **his** newspapers for recycling.

Common pronouns: he, she, it, they, him, her, them, his, hers, theirs.

First person narrative: a character tells the story as well as being in it.

I go to school early so that **I** can hand in **my** newspapers for recycling.

Common pronouns: I, we, me, us, mine, ours.

Tip

Pronouns stand in for people or objects to avoid repetition.

Example: The duck said that the duck gave the duck's mum a present. The duck said that **she** gave **her** mum a present.

B  **Use possessive pronouns and adjectives.**

Language focus

Possessive pronouns and possessive adjectives do different jobs.
Possessive adjectives appear with the noun they modify.
Possessive pronouns take the place of a noun.
Example:

That's **my** <u>egg</u>, not your <u>egg</u>. → That <u>egg</u> is **mine**, not **yours**.

    possessive adjective   possessive pronoun

Personal pronoun	Possessive adjectives	Possessive pronouns
I	my	mine
you	your	yours
he	his	his
she	her	hers
it	its	-
we	our	ours
they	their	theirs

1 Choose the correct word for these sentences.

   a The ant carried (*her/hers*) load on (*her/hers*) back.

   b The ants said, "This corn is (*our/ours*)."

   c Please share (*your/yours*) food with me.

   d People should not steal what is not (*their/theirs*).

   e Why don't you come and warm up at (*my/mine*) house?

2 Replace the personal pronoun (*I, you, he/she/it, we, they*) with the correct possessive adjective or pronoun.

   a Winter made (*it*) presence felt.

   b We are collecting food for (*we*) stores.

   c All the food I have collected should be (*I*).

   d They gave me (*they*) word.

   e All that I have is (*you*).

Ⓒ 📖 💬 📝 **Not everyone sees things the same way. How might the story change if Ant or Grasshopper was telling it?**

One fine summer's day, deep in a meadow, I noticed a grasshopper bouncing about, chirruping and singing without a care in the world ...

One fine summer's day, deep in a meadow, I was bouncing about, chirruping and singing without a care in the world ...

1 Decide with a talk partner who will tell the story from Ant's and Grasshopper's points-of-view.

2 Re-read the story and decide what to change to make your character the narrator. You can also change some story details.

- What does Ant really think about Grasshopper?
- What does Grasshopper really think about Ant?

3 Make notes of your changes.

4 Tell each other the story from your character's point-of-view.

5 Proverbs tell a tale

A 📖💬 **Stories can help us to learn tricky lessons about life; we remember the story, so we remember the lesson.**

> A proverb is a memorable saying that gives advice or a life lesson – for example: *Never judge a duck by his feathers!*

1 In a small group, read the proverbs below and explain to each other what they mean.

- Never put off until tomorrow what you can do today.
- A friend in need is a friend indeed.
- Do as you would be done by.

2 *Make hay while the sun shines* is a **figurative** expression. Use the pictures on page 15 to help you discuss what it means **literally** and then work out the lesson that it teaches.

Tip

A dictionary gives you the **literal** meaning of a word. **Figurative** descriptions use images to express meaning. We **infer** the meaning from the images.

3 Which of the proverbs in question 1 has the same meaning as *Make hay while the sun shines*?

> I'm no dab hand at farming but I know it's easier catching fish in good weather ... never put off until tomorrow ...

infer *v.* to work out using prior knowledge

B 📝 **Design a cartoon strip to illustrate a proverb.**

1 Choose one of the proverbs and tell each other an idea for a scenario that could teach the lesson in the proverb.

2 Plan a cartoon strip of your scenario. Sketch the scene and write dialogue in the speech bubbles.

3 Add any necessary narrative text. Keep it brief.

4 Complete the cartoon strip and share it with the class.

Any volunteers? Who'd like to share their cartoon?

6 A twist in the traditional tale

A 📖 💬 **Explore a modern version of the fable.**

1 Look at the story on the next page. This version of the fable is titled *Auntie Anthea and Gentle Geoffrey*. Which is the Ant and which is the Grasshopper? How could you tell?

2 Predict how this modern retelling (from the title and the pictures) might be similar to or different from the traditional version.

B 📖 💬 **The story can be read in groups of three.**

1 Skim the story to identify the narrator: is it Geoffrey, Anthea or a third person narrator?

2 Read the story together. List similarities and differences between this and the previous version.

Auntie Anthea and Gentle Geoffrey

Summer had been a blast and Gentle Geoffrey had loved every minute. He felt so inspired and his music was sweeter than ever. Auntie Anthea had also enjoyed the summer. Gentle Geoffrey's music had certainly made cleaning and collecting food seem much less effort.

As the weather cooled, Gentle Geoffrey's chirruping became a little less cheerful. Auntie Anthea, on the other hand, was still scrubbing and storing, although it seemed a little more of a chore.

By the time the winter chill set in, Geoffrey felt famished and frail. He'd played music all summer with his head in the clouds, so he had no home to go to and no food to eat. But just as he thought he should do something, he caught a faint melody in the whistling wind and once more could think of little else. Auntie Anthea, meanwhile, was warm and well-fed but was finding winter dull, with little to liven up her diet and daily chores. All of a sudden, she thought of Geoffrey.

"What a tasty treat!" she clapped.
"I adore insects and Geoffrey will make a delicious difference. He never knows what's what with all that music filling his head. He'll leap at the chance of filling his tummy and I've never grazed on a grasshopper before."

"A … A … Auntie Anthea," shivered Geoffrey, surprised to see her braving the frosty fields. "Wh … wh … whaddya you doing here?"

"I couldn't help thinking of you turning into a block of ice out here," said Anthea, trying to keep the anticipation in her voice at bay. "I want a tenant, and who could be more delicious, I mean delightful, than you?"

"D … d … delicious? That doesn't sound so c … c … cool. I think I'll g … g … give it a miss, if it's all the s … s … same to you," quavered Geoffrey.

"Well, it's not – my heart's set on you taking you home for supper," lured Anthea. "Just come on inside for a bit."

"A b … b … bit of what?"

"A bit of a bite, of course!" snapped Anthea, with a touch of irritation.

"But a b … b … bite of wh … wh … what?" Geoffrey worried as he crumpled to the ground, too weak to stand.

Anthea dashed forward, slung Geoffrey onto her back, hauled him home and laid him in front of the fire, licking her lips in anticipation. Geoffrey, revived by the warmth, thought for a moment and then smiled winningly at Anthea.

"Auntie, the other insects said you were, well, mean, but you seem so kind. What can I, you know, do, um, to thank you for your hospitality?"

"Well, I had thought …" Anthea trailed off, hoping her tummy wasn't rumbling too obviously.

"Hmmm! I'd rather sing for my supper than be your supper," Geoffrey declared, and he began to sing, softly at first but gaining in strength with every note. Anthea loved it and suddenly realised what was really good about having Gentle Geoffrey in her home. She could cook and clean and he could keep her company and entertain her friends. Now that would be a giant leap forward for antkind!

Sally Burt

Did you know?

Geoffrey is a name with English, French and German origins. It means 'peace'. Do you think it was a good name for the grasshopper in this story?

C 👥 **Prepare a short group presentation summarising this version of the story.**

1 Use your notes and the questions below to prepare your presentation.

 a What are Anthea and Geoffrey like? What are their talents?

 b What does Anthea intend for Geoffrey at first?

 c What does she say that makes Geoffrey reluctant to go with her?

 d What shows that Geoffrey knows what Anthea is planning?

 e What do you think of his solution to the problem?

 f What is the twist in the tale?

 g What lesson does this fable teach?

 h Which version of the story do you prefer and why?

2 Give your group presentation to the class.

Answer any questions when you have finished.

Why not think of a few questions you might like to ask other groups in advance? Never put off until tomorrow ...

How did I do?

- Did we use evidence to explain our comments?
- Did we explain clearly which version we prefer?
- Did we make sure everyone takes part in a discussion?

D 📝 Add *Auntie Anthea and Gentle Geoffrey* to your reading log.
Note down whether you preferred this version or the original.

7 It's all about dialogue

A 📖 💬 Learn about punctuating direct speech.

Language focus

Punctuating dialogue

- Put speech marks before and after the spoken words.
- Capitalise the first word inside the speech marks.
- Use a comma after any words introducing the speech.
- Start a new line when a new person speaks.
- If the narrative indicating who spoke (e.g. *she said*) comes **after** the speech, put the comma, exclamation mark or question mark (never a full stop) before closing the speech marks with no capital letter for the word that follows.

comma after words that introduce the speech

punctuation inside the speech marks

Anthea said, "I love insects!"
"Not me, I hope," whispered Geoffrey.

new line for each speaker

capital letter

punctuation inside the speech marks

no capital letter

1 Scan the story to locate the punctuation showing dialogue.

   a Does it follow the rules on the previous page?

   b Can you write any other rules to guide you?

2 Discuss how the punctuation works in the sentence below:

"Auntie Anthea," said Geoffrey, "why are you here?"

3 Write these sentences into your notebook, adding the speech marks, correct punctuation and using interesting verbs to show how the characters speak.

But you eat insects.

You shouldn't believe everything you hear!

Why else would you want me to come to your house?

Well, the pantry is nice and warm ...

B 📝 **Extend the story.**

1 Continue the conversation between Geoffrey and Anthea after Geoffrey finishes singing.

   a Write at least two more things for each character.

   b Keep the dialogue 'in character'.

   c Use the correct punctuation for the dialogue and the narrative.

2 Check you have used descriptive verbs in place of *said, asked* or *replied*.

C 👥 **Do a dramatic reading of the dialogue in the story, including your new dialogue.**

1 Practise reading out only the dialogue with a talk partner.

2 Use the narrative and the way the words are written to help you understand how to put across your ideas about the characters. Support your interpretation with speech and gesture.

Any volunteers?
Who'd like to do a dramatic reading in character?

8 Figurative language

A 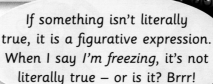 **Figures of speech are all around us in our everyday language.**

1 Discuss these expressions in a small group.

    a Do you know these expressions?

    b What do they mean literally?

    c How you might use them in everyday speech?

> under the weather   spill the beans
> give me a break   read between the lines
> take a rain check   on the ball
> back to square one

2 Choose three of the expressions and use each one in a sentence.

If something isn't literally true, it is a figurative expression. When I say I'm freezing, it's not literally true — or is it? Brrr!

3 Think up some other figurative expressions you know.

    a In your group, choose one figurative expression each.

    b Each draw a **literal** picture to illustrate your expression.

    c Swap your pictures with another group and guess each other's expressions.

4 Find the following figurative expressions in the passage.

    a Discuss what they mean literally.

    b Discuss what they mean figuratively in the context of the story.

      • *summer had been a blast*

      • *with his head in the clouds*

      • *that doesn't sound c … c … cool*

5 In the first version of the fable, Grasshopper's song *stuck in his throat* when winter came. What does this expression mean, both literally and figuratively? How do you think it came about?

6 Geoffrey tells Anthea he would rather *sing for his supper* than **be** her supper. Is he using the expression figuratively or literally? Why?

B 💬 **Alliteration is a figure of speech because the effect of the repeated consonant sound makes the words more memorable.**

1 Discuss the effect of alliteration in the names of the characters.

    a Does it suit their characters?

    b Invent an alternative name for each character using alliteration.

2 Think of a word that alliterates with your name and reflects something about you.

3 Anthea often uses alliteration in her speech.

    a Identify three examples of alliteration in her dialogue.

    b How does alliteration make the words stand out?

4 Find three more examples of alliteration in the story. What effect does it have?

9 Hold a discussion forum

A 💬👥 **Fables are part of the oral tradition; the same story often has different versions, details or endings.**

1 In groups of four, discuss an alternative ending to one of the versions of the fable.

2 Prepare a group presentation to include:

    a which fable you have chosen

    b your thoughts on the discussion points given below

    c an alternative ending to the fable

    d the lesson to be learned from your alternative ending.

> Remember, in group work, you share out the work – many hands make light work!

The original version:	The modern version:
• What happened to Grasshopper at the end?	• What happened to Geoffrey at the end?
• What did Ant do about it?	• What did Anthea do when Geoffrey was cold and hungry?
• Do you think this was right?	• Do you think this was right?
• Was Grasshopper lazy?	• Was Geoffrey lazy?
• What could Ant or Grasshopper have done to change the outcome?	• Was Anthea a good friend to Geoffrey?
• Explain how the fable could be changed to teach the lesson *A friend in need is a friend indeed*?	• How could the lesson *One good turn deserves another* apply to this fable?

3 Give your presentations and discuss each other's ideas.

- Listen carefully during the presentation.
- Ask questions after the presentation.
- Be prepared to offer your ideas but accept others' different ideas too.

10 Test your knowledge

A 📖 **Read a story from India independently.**

1 Skim read the story to get the main idea.

2 Summarise the main idea for yourself in one or two sentences.

Three Fish – A Tale from India

Three fish lived in a pond. One was named Plan Ahead, another was Think Fast, and the third was named Wait and See. One day they heard a fisherman say that he was going to cast his net in their pond the next day.

Plan Ahead said, "I'm swimming down the river tonight!"

Think Fast said, "I'm sure I'll come up with a plan."

Wait and See lazily said, "I just can't think about it now!"

When the fisherman cast his nets, Plan Ahead was long gone. But Think Fast and Wait and See were caught.

Think Fast quickly rolled his belly up and pretended to be dead. "Oh, this fish is no good!" said the fisherman, and threw him safely back into the water. But Wait and See ended up in the fish market.

That is why they say, "In times of danger, when the net is cast, plan ahead or plan to think fast!"

Retold by Heather Forest

B **Use headings to help you summarise a story.**

Remember, there were three fish so you will need three solutions!

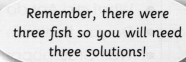

1 Make notes under each heading.

Setting	Characters	Problem	Solutions	Ending	Lesson

2 Write a short paragraph explaining whether you would classify *The Three Fish* as a fable. Use evidence from the text to support your view.

How did I do?

- Can I recognise fable features?
- Can I explain my point-of-view clearly?
- Can I use evidence from the story to support my views?

11 and 12 Retelling a fable

A 🗨 📝 **Retelling a familiar story is fun. You don't have to think too hard about the plot because you already know it!**

1 Plan a retelling of either *The Ant and the Grasshopper* or *The Three Fish*. Keep the key features of a fable, but change something, for example:
   - choose different characters or a different setting
   - write a different ending to the fable
   - use the same characters but teach a different lesson.

2 Use a planning diagram to make notes.

Section 1 Characters and setting	Section 2 Problem/Issue	Section 3 How the issue works out	Section 4 Lesson to be learned

Short, simple story ✓
Animal characters who act like humans ✓
Dialogue shows their characteristics ✓
Figurative language or alliteration ✓
Character learns a lesson ✓
We can also learn a lesson ✓

3 Swap plans with a talk partner. Can you tell each other's story aloud, using the plan?

4 Has your partner included the key features of a fable? Suggest improvements.

5 Adapt your plan if necessary.

B 📝 **Write your fable from your plan.**

1 Write a first draft, section by section.

2 Use the editing checklist to review your work. Then ask your talk partner to read it for flow, sense and originality.

3 Finalise your story and illustrate it to emphasise what has changed from the original.

C 👥 **Make a class anthology of your fables and read them aloud to friends and family.**

Don't forget to start a new line each time a different character starts to speak.

Tip

Rememeber to check your work for mistakes.

2 Exploring space

In this unit you'll find out what it's like to explore space by reading about people's experiences in biographies, journals and interviews. You'll research, summarise and order information, ask good questions and write a biography and an imaginary space journal of your own.

Vocabulary to learn and use:
astronomy, astronauts, cosmonauts, observatory, orbit, spacecraft, telescope, biography, journal

1 What is 'out there'?

A 📖 💬 **Read about how our knowledge of space has grown. Then discuss the questions on page 26.**

A brief history of astronomy

The first star catalogue was completed by the Greek <u>astronomer</u> Hipparchus in 129 BCE.

That was clever, without a telescope!

In 1543 the Polish astronomer Nicolaus Copernicus claimed that the Earth moved around the Sun!

In those days everyone thought the Sun moved around the Earth!

Danishman Tycho Brahe was a famous <u>naked-eye</u> astronomer. He built the world's leading <u>observatory</u> in Uraniborg in 1576.

The first telescopes were probably made by spectacle-makers in the early 1600s. They made distant objects appear closer.

In 1609, the Italian scientist, Galileo, built a telescope that allowed him to view sunspots and the moons of Jupiter. In 1613, he used his observations to prove Copernicus's theory correct.

In 1704, the English scientist Isaac Newton designed a reflector telescope with greater <u>magnification</u> and a clearer image than earlier telescopes.

The idea of a telescope in space was suggested by an American astronomer, Lyman Spitzer, in 1946.

In 1957, the USSR launched the first <u>artificial</u> **satellite**, *Sputnik 1*, into space.

satellite *n.* a natural or man-made object that orbits another object

So the space race was on! Who would be the first to send a human into space?

On 12th April 1961, Russian Cosmonaut Yuri Gagarin became the first man in space.

The first woman in space was Russian cosmonaut Valentina Tereshkova in 1963.

Did you know?

The term *astronaut* refers to members of the NASA space programme. The term *cosmonaut* refers to members of the Russian space programme.

Buzz was a childhood nickname – his real name was Edwin!

On 20th July 1969, American astronauts Neil Armstrong and Buzz Aldrin became the first people to walk on the Moon.

In 2000, the first crew moved into the International Space Station which was finally completed in 2011.

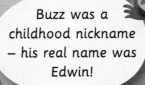

They don't stay at the ISS for too long. Can you imagine why?

1 Discuss as a class.

   a Do you recognise the names of any of these people or places?

   b Which significant event made space exploration possible?

   c People from different nations have contributed to the field of astronomy. Name some of these nations.

   d What new facts did you discover from this information?

   e What questions do you have about this topic?

B 📝💬 **A timeline is a summary of events in sequence.**

1 In your notebook, make a timeline to show the order of these events. Use key words only e.g. dates and names.

2 Take turns with a talk partner to explain a brief history of space exploration using your timeline.

C 📖📝**AZ** **You can often work out the meanings of words and abbreviations from the context.**

1 Use the context to work out the meaning of the underlined words in the text. Write down your own definition and then use a dictionary to check if you're right.

astronomer
naked-eye
observatory
magnification
artificial

2 An abbreviation is a shortened form of a word or phrase using a few of the letters of the original word, or the initial letters. Can you work out what these abbreviations from the text stand for?

USSR NASA ISS BCE

2 Building sentences

A **A sentence is the basic building block for writing.**

Language focus

Sentences should:
- contain a (finite) verb
- make sense on their own
- begin with a capital letter
- end with a full stop, question mark or exclamation mark
- have question words for questions or command verbs for instructions.

<u>Simple sentences</u> have a **subject** (who or what is doing the action), a **verb** (the action) and deal with **one idea**.

<u>Compound sentences</u> are formed by joining simple sentences with a conjunction e.g. *and, for, but, so, or, yet, if.*

1   In your notebook, complete each sentence by filling in the subject.
    Example: Hipparchus <u>completed</u> the first
                 scientific star catalogue. (Who?)

    Tip
    To find the subject underline the verb and ask *who* or *what* is doing the action.

    a ? invented the first telescopes.
    b ? moves around the Sun.
    c ? designed a reflector telescope.
    d The first person to walk on the Moon was ?

2   Join two simple sentences with an appropriate conjunction. Write the compound sentences in your notebook. You can leave out any unnecessary words to make your sentence sound more natural.
    Example: A satellite is a natural object. A satellite is a man-made object.
                 A satellite is a natural or man-made object.

    a Early astronomers observed the stars.
       They observed the Moon.
    b Copernicus made a major discovery.
       Nobody believed him.

    Tip
    Remember – two simple sentences joined together form a compound sentence.

c Galileo developed the telescope.

He did not invent it.

d Astronauts can work in space.

They can work on the ground.

B 📖 ✍ **Use adverbs and adverbial phrases to improve sentences.**

Language focus

Adverbials are single words or groups of words that add information about the verb, saying when, where or how the action takes place. Adverbial phrases of time describe when the action takes place. For example:

The astronaut blasted off into space.

After many hours of preparation, the astronaut blasted off into space.

> I think the second sentence is more interesting.

1 Read the history of astronomy text again and note down the adverbial phrases of time that tell us *when* the events occurred.

Example: On 12th April 1961

2 Use your timeline to write five sentences using some of these adverbial phrases of time to show the order of events.

> Long before ...   Finally ...
> For the first time ...   Then ...
> After that ...   Eventually ...
> In the early 1600s ...
> After Galileo's invention ...
> Many years later ...
> In 1969 ...

How did I do?

- Did I order events on a timeline?
- Did I identify the subject in a simple sentence?
- Did I join two simple sentences?
- Did I use adverbs and adverbial phrases of time to improve a sentence?

A 📖 📝 **AZ** **A biography tells you about a person's life.**

1 Read the biographies below to find out about some astronomy 'firsts'.

Yuri Gagarin

The Huntsville Times

Man Enters Space

'So Close, Yet So Far,' Sighs Cape
U.S. Had Hoped For Own Launch

Soviet Officer Orbits Globe In 5-Ton Ship
Maximum Height Reached Reported As 188 Miles

Hobbs Admits 1844 Slaying

Dates

9th March 1934–27th March 1968

Childhood

Yuri Gagarin was born in Klushino, a small village west of Moscow, the third of four children. Growing up during World War II, life was difficult. His father worked as a carpenter and bricklayer and his mother worked as a milkmaid.

Training for the future

In school, Yuri was good at mathematics and physics. After school, he discovered a love of flying and joined the Soviet Air Force. He enjoyed being a fighter pilot, but he really wanted to go to space.

First cosmonaut

In 1960, he was one of 20 applicants chosen to be the Soviet Union's first <u>cosmonaut</u>. Gagarin remained calm under the pressure of the intense training and <u>excelled</u> at the tasks, while also keeping his sense of humour. Later, he was chosen to be the first man into space because of these skills. It also helped that he was short and could fit into a small space capsule!

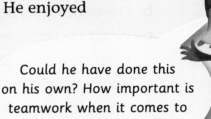

Could he have done this on his own? How important is teamwork when it comes to great achievements?

Lift-off

On 12th April 1961, at 9:07 a.m. *Vostok 1* was launched. Just after lift-off, Gagarin is said to have called out, *Poyekhali!* ('Off we go!'). He was rocketed into space and completed a single <u>orbit</u> around Earth.

Mission <u>accomplished</u>

At the end of the orbit, *Vostok 1* re-entered the Earth's atmosphere. Gagarin <u>ejected</u> (as planned) from the spacecraft and used a parachute to land safely – just 108 minutes after blast off. Yuri Gagarin became both the first person to enter space and the first person to orbit the Earth.

Imagine volunteering for that job! How do you think he felt?

Tycho Brahe

Dates: 1546–1601

He gained fame as a young astronomer. In 1575, King Frederick II gave him an island and financial support to build an observatory. Here he made accurate observations and precise measurements of the planets before the invention of the telescope!

Valentina Tereshkova

Dates: 1937–

She was the first woman in space. After her 1963 mission she became involved in politics. She has been awarded many honours and prizes for her achievements. A crater on the far side of the Moon is named after her!

Laika

Dates: 1953–1957

This Russian space dog became the first animal to orbit the Earth in November 1957. Laika travelled in a spacecraft known as *Sputnik 2. Laika* means 'barker' in Russian, and her mission helped scientists understand whether people could survive in space.

2 Can you work out the meanings of the underlined words? Write down your definitions and then check them using a dictionary.

3 Answer these questions in your notebook.

   a In which country was Yuri Gagarin born?

   b Describe Yuri's childhood.

   c What characteristics and skills made him suitable for the job of cosmonaut?

   d How long did his first mission last?

   e How old was Yuri at the time of his first mission?

   f How could Tycho Brahe afford to build an observatory?

   g Why are Valentina Tereshkova's dates incomplete?

   h What can you tell from the dates on Laika's biography?

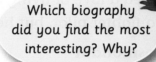

Which biography did you find the most interesting? Why?

B 💬 **Compare features of biographies.**

1 Compare and discuss these features of the biographies.

   a the purpose

   b the tense

   c the order of the information

   d how headings are used to organise the text

   e narrative.

C 📝 **Update your reading log to show that you have read a biography.**

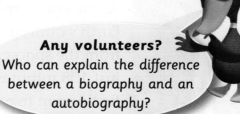

Any volunteers?
Who can explain the difference between a biography and an autobiography?

5 Making links

A **Every text has a structure. When a text is organised into paragraphs, a topic sentence helps to link them.**

1 Why do you think a text is divided into paragraphs?

2 Identify the topic sentence of each paragraph in the biography of Yuri Gagarin. Write them out in your notebook.

Tip

Read the first sentence of each paragraph!

3 What is the rest of each paragraph about? Summarise them under the topic sentences, using key words and phrases only.

4 Use your summary to tell your talk partner about Yuri Gagarin.

How does a topic sentence link each paragraph to the main topic?

B **One way to get your writing to flow and make sense is to use adverbials.**

Language focus

Adverbials tell us when, where or how the action takes place. They can be single words (adverbs) or groups of words (adverbial phrases or adverbial clauses). Adverbials can move to different positions to highlight different parts of the sentence. For example:

adverbial clause

She became involved in politics <u>after she completed her 1963 mission</u>.
<u>After she completed her 1963 mission</u>, she became involved in politics.

When the adverbial clause starts the sentence, it's handy to use a comma to help make sense of the sentence.

Tip

Remember:

● a **phrase** is a group of words without a verb:
  after that

● a **clause** is a group of words with a finite verb:
  after <u>she completed</u> her mission

1 Move the underlined adverbial clause from the end to the beginning of each sentence.

   a Yuri Gagarin had a difficult life <u>while he was growing up</u>.

   b He discovered a love of flying <u>after he finished school</u>.

   c Gagarin kept his calm <u>while he completed his training</u>.

   d Gagarin called out, *Poyekhali!* <u>soon after the lift-off occurred</u>.

   e *Vostok 1* re-entered the Earth's atmosphere <u>when it had finished orbiting the Earth</u>.

C 📝 💬 **AZ** **Many words in English originate from words in other languages such as Greek, Latin and French.**

1 The following root words or prefixes came from Greek words. Can you work out what they mean? Find a good match for each one.

bio	far off or from afar
auto	outer space
astro	by oneself
cosmo	life
tele	star

2 Find words with these word origins. Use a dictionary.

How did I do?

- Did I identify features of a biography?
- Did I find information in a biography?
- Did I identify and explain what a topic sentence is?
- Did I use adverbials of time and re-order sentences?

6 The past tense

A 📝 **AZ** **A biography is written using the past tense because it is about things that have happened in a person's life in the past.**

1 In your notebook, write down the past tense of the verbs to complete these sentences.

   a He (*gain*) fame as a young astronomer.

   b Laika (*travel*) in a spacecraft known as *Sputnik 2*.

c In school, Yuri (*love*) mathematics and physics.

d After school, he (*discover*) a love of flying and joined the Soviet Air Force.

e During the intense training Gagarin (*excel*) while keeping his calm.

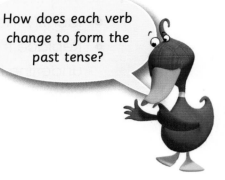

How does each verb change to form the past tense?

2 Irregular verbs do not follow the usual spelling patterns when changing tenses. Identify the irregular verb in each sentence and discuss how they are irregular.

a A Russian space dog became the first animal to orbit the Earth.

b He made accurate observations and precise measurements.

c King Frederick II gave him an island and financial support.

3 In your notebook, write these sentences in the past tense using an irregular verb.

a Tycho chooses to study astronomy at university.

b He begins a career as an astronomer and becomes famous.

c Brahe builds an enormous observatory.

d Yuri Gagarin dreams of going into space.

e The astronauts speed towards the Moon.

B 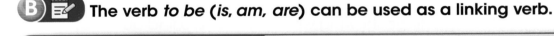 **The verb *to be* (*is, am, are*) can be used as a linking verb.**

Language focus

As a linking verb, the verb *to be* can be written:

- Put in the past tense form (*was, were*)
- using pronouns
- to connect a noun (or pronoun) with another noun
- to connect a noun (or pronoun) with an adjective.

noun + noun:

Neil Armstrong (He) was <u>an astronomer</u>.

noun (or pronoun) verb   noun

Remember: a singular subject needs a singular verb and a plural subject needs a plural verb.

noun + adjective:

Neil and Buzz (They) were <u>happy</u> to go to the Moon.

noun (or pronoun) verb adjective

1 Rewrite these sentences in your notebook, following the instructions.
   - Identify the word that comes from the verb *to be*.
   - Replace the underlined noun with a third person pronoun and underline it.
   - State if the verb connects two nouns (n+n) or if it connects a noun and an adjective (n+a).
     Example: Laika is a dog.
     She (was) a dog (n+n)
   a Valentina Tereshkova was well-prepared for her first mission.
   b The early astronomers were observers of the skies.
   c Tycho Brahe is famous for his measurements of the planets.
   d The Earth is a planet orbiting the Sun.
   e Some astronomers are fighter-pilots.

7 and 8 Plan and write a biography

A Of all the people you've learned about so far in this unit, who did you find most interesting? Is there someone else you would like to know about?

1 Write three or four headings showing what you want to find out about your chosen person, for example:

   Childhood   Training   Achievements   Other interests

2 In groups, research information about their life. Pool your information and resources.
3 Now work on your own. Note the information you find under your headings. Write key words and phrases only.
4 In your own words, write a short biography about the person.
   - Don't write more than 50 words per paragraph.
   - Your biography must be written in the past tense.
   - Write in the third person.
5 Ask your partner for feedback and then edit your work.
6 Write your biography neatly on a sheet of paper for display.
   Try to include some pictures.
7 Share your work with the class by displaying your biography.

Use criteria to assess each other's work and give some positive feedback!

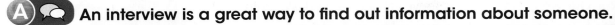

9 and 10 Discuss interviews

A 💬 **An interview is a great way to find out information about someone.**

1 What rules or 'manners' are **employed** in an interview?
2 What tips would you give to someone being interviewed or giving an interview?

> **employ** *v.* to give a person a job; to use something

> Who can explain what an interview is and what it's for?

Did you know?

The person being interviewed is the **interviewee** and the person giving the interview is the **interviewer**.

> What do you miss most in space?

> Swimming!

> NEWS

B 💬 👥 **Using modern technology, school space programs can sometimes arrange for schoolchildren to interview astronauts in space. In the following interview, children spoke to astronaut Chris Cassidy on board the International Space Station (ISS).**

1 Work with a partner. Read the interview (on page 36) aloud, taking one role each.

Did you know?

Different languages are spoken on board the ISS including 'Runglish' which is a mixture of languages. Can you guess which languages they are?

Hi Chris, my name is Rui. Can you tell us what happens to your waste water on the ISS?

Hi Rui. Our water on the ISS is recycled and reused. We collect it in plastic bags, standard refuse around here! And it gets processed through a special system. So we reuse it the next day!

My name is Carlos. If you could change a part of the design or layout on the ISS, what would it be?

That's a really good question, Carlos. I would definitely add more windows. We have a couple here and I'm looking down on Earth as we speak, but I think you can never have enough windows.

Hello Chris! My name is Cindy. I'd like to know if there are ever any misunderstandings between the ISS crew members?

That's an interesting point, Cindy. Misunderstandings are usually language-related because we have to communicate in other languages. We might get our words mixed up or say something that doesn't make sense. This can actually be quite funny.

Hi, my name is Sam. What do you do in your spare time on the ISS?

Hi Sam. Our personal space on the ISS is about the size of a refrigerator, so our activities are limited. I really enjoy looking out of the window, chatting to my family once a day and spending time with the crew.

 Ask good interview questions.

1 A 'space interview' usually lasts about ten minutes. Children have to prepare their questions beforehand. Why?

2 Compare the following pairs of questions. Which one draws out the most information? Explain why.

   a Do you enjoy being an astronaut?
   What do you enjoy about being an astronaut?

   b What type of training did you have to go through?
   Was your training very difficult?

   c Do you have plans for the future?
   What plans do you have for the future?

   d Did you always want to be an astronaut?
   How did you become an astronaut?

Do you like swimming?

Yes.

What are your favourite activities and why?

Well now, let's see ...

3 Imagine you could interview an astronaut in space. In your notebook, write five questions that you would like to ask.

4 Share your questions with a partner. Has your partner used question words and the correct punctuation? Give each other positive feedback.

Tip

Use question words like 'why?' and 'how?' to make sure your questions open up a topic and give the interviewee a chance to explain or describe something.

D **Use role play to express what you have learned.**

1 Choose and role play one of these options with a partner. You can take turns to be the interviewer and the interviewee.

a An interview with an **imaginary** astronaut. Use information in this unit to plan questions and make up suitable answers.

b An interview with a **real** person. You can use the Yuri Gagarin biography or any other personal account to plan your questions and find answers.

Don't forget to keep eye contact and speak clearly. Use good expression to keep the attention of your audience!

How did I do?

● Did I change sentences into the past tense?
● Did I plan and write a biography?
● Did I ask and answer questions in an interview?

11 Read and compare journals

A 💬 📝 **Personal writing is writing we do for a personal reason. Sometimes this writing is private and sometimes it is for others to read.**

1 Think about different types of personal writing.

2 a What kinds of personal writing do you enjoy doing?

   b If you found a letter or a diary belonging to someone else, would you read it?

   c Would you be happy if someone read your diary?

   d When is a diary or journal not meant to be private?

3 Many early astronomers kept journals to record their research, observations and discoveries. Galileo's 1610 journal shows sketches of the objects around Jupiter which he later recognised to be moons.

Wow! That's over 400 years ago!

   a Can you imagine the kinds of things that Galileo may have written in his journal?

   b Was there any other way, in those days, to record this information?

   c What other ways of recording events and experiences do we have now?

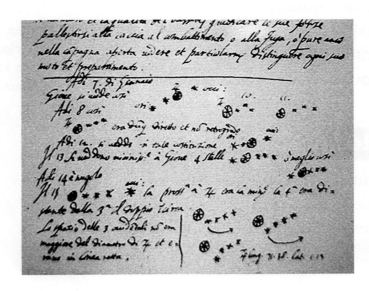

B 📖 💬 📝 **Blogs and tweets are a modern form of journal writing. Today we can keep up-to-date with everyday life in space by reading tweets and blogs written by people living on the ISS.**

1 Read some tweets from astronauts in space or in training.

    a What activities are part of an astronaut's job?

    b How do these astronauts feel about what they do?

    c Does an astronaut's job sound like something you would enjoy?

Sunita Williams   21 Jul

Saturday morning on the International Space Station - cleaning!!

■ **View photo** ▸ **Retweet** ★ **Favourite**

Chris Hadfield   10 May

What a fun day! This type of event is what the years of training were for. A happy, busy crew, working hard, loving life in space.

■ **View photo** ▸ **Retweet** ★ **Favourite**

Tim Peake   1 Dec

Scuba diving today in NASA's enormous 12 m deep pool ... Space station mock-up is used for spacewalk training – great fun!

■ **View photo** ▸ **Retweet** ★ **Favourite**

Sam Christoforetti   17 Jul

I've just been to space and back ... nominal ascent and re-entry profiles in the 18 m centrifuge – very interesting!

■ **View photo** ▸ **Retweet** ★ **Favourite**

Sam Christoforetti   16 Jul

While I was in training @Astro_Luca was fighting w/water leaking in helmet. A pity #EVA had to be terminated, but so good everyone is fine!

■ **View photo** ▸ **Retweet** ★ **Favourite**

2 A blog is a type of journal. Read a blog by astronaut Sunita Williams who has lived on the International Space Station.

Life on the ISS:

Well, it has been a busy week! The main event was the arrival of the *Progress* **resupply craft**. The long wait was well worth it. Once the spacecraft was secured, we **equalised** the pressure and cracked open the hatch. 'Gorby' (our nickname for the *Progress*) was overflowing with exciting goodies for us. Not only did we get fresh food like apples, tomatoes and oranges (just love that smell) but also chocolate (lots of it!). It's great to eat fresh food again, I automatically feel healthier.

We also got some cards and gifts from FFF (family, friends and fans) back home. Everyone took a little time to themselves to sit back, read and enjoy the news (though old) from home.

Other activities this week:
- A computer reload. It went well with the expert help from our ground team. Well done everyone!
- Our usual daily exercise routine of biking, running and pushing weights. Don't think you can even miss one day up here! We have to keep our muscles working or they will forget what to do!
- We spoke to the International Space School in Scotland! Their questions were great and they invited me to visit them next summer! I can't wait.
- And finally, my favourite! It was my turn to clean the station this week ...

Here's one of our crew, Cosmonaut Fyodor N. Yurchikhin, juggling our fresh cargo! Not much skill required since those oranges just hang in the air!

resupply craft *n.* a spacecraft with no crew that delivers supplies to the space station and removes waste
equalise *v.* to make or become equal

3 a What period of time does this journal cover?

  b What activities are mentioned in the blog?

  c Why is the news from home described as *old*?

  d Is this journal public or private? How do you know?

  e Find examples of **colloquial** language in the blog.

  f What factual information does it include?

> **colloquial** *adj.* informal

4 Does Sunita Williams use more than one tense in her journal? Give examples.

C ✎ **Update your reading log to show that you have read a modern journal or blog.**

> **Tip**
>
> Be creative! You could make it look like a computer blog or your own personal journal.

12 Write a journal or blog

A ✎ **Life on the ISS sounds like a mixture of hard work and fun. Imagine being on the ISS for a week! Write an astronaut's blog or journal.**

1 Read a list of some of the jobs that the astronauts have to do.

> Maintain equipment; do a spacewalk outside the station to check and repair equipment; conduct scientific experiments; exercise daily for about two hours; update ground control; take photographs of the Earth; enjoy some free time to read and make contact with family.

2 Plan a journal or blog covering your imaginary week as an astronaut. Include the above activities, your personal thoughts and experiences.

  a Organise your journal into headings and sections.

  b Include factual information *and* personal opinions.

  c Use friendly language with a few colloquial terms.

  d Remember to use varying tenses according to your purpose. Use the past tense to describe things that you did and felt before. Use the present tense to describe what you are doing and feeling now. Use the future tense to describe what you will do later.

  e Use adverbial phrases and clauses of time to sequence the events.

  f Remember to include specialised 'space' terms and vocabulary.

3 Share your draft with a partner and get some feedback. Edit and correct your work.

4 Create a final version of your journal for display. Include pictures, diagrams and personal notes from friends and family.

3 Reflections

Nature is something we all experience in different ways. Over the centuries, poets have expressed their experiences of nature in a wide range of poetic forms. In this unit you'll read and compare rhyming poems, haikus and free verse nature poems. You will write your own haiku and choose a poem to perform.

Vocabulary to learn and use:
haiku, reflection, nature, obvious, subtle, analyse, personification, comparison, simile, metaphor, structure, contrast, atmosphere

1 Listen and discuss

A Sometimes, listening helps us to focus, reflect and imagine.
Listen to your teacher read the poem.

1 **a** What is it about?
   b Who is the 'voice' in the poem?
   c What do you think about the poem? Did you enjoy it?

Who Has Seen the Wind?

Who has seen the wind?
Neither I nor you:
But when the leaves hang trembling
The wind is passing through.

Who has seen the wind?
Neither you nor I:
But when the trees bow down their heads
The wind is passing by.

Christina Rossetti

Did you know?

Christina Rossetti (1830–94) was educated at home in England by her mother. A keen learner from the start, she dictated her first story to her mother before she could write!

B 📝 💬 **Many poets are inspired by nature. There are poems about plants and animals, the seasons, the sea and many more natural topics.**

1 Have you ever been surprised, scared or amazed by something you've seen in nature?

2 How do you feel about things in nature? Think up some words that describe your experience of these things.

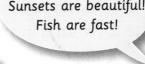

> Storms are scary!
> Sunsets are beautiful!
> Fish are fast!

> the sun   the rain   summer   winter   night time

Share your ideas with the class. Others might feel differently from you. Explore the differences.

3 Two poems about the same thing are never alike. Why do you think that is?

C 📖 📝 **The form or structure of a poem can add to our enjoyment.**

1 Re-read the poem on your own and answer the questions in your notebook.

   a How does the first line get your attention?

   b How many stanzas are there?

   c How many lines are there?

   d Which lines are repeated?

   e What is the rhyming pattern?

> **Any volunteers?**
> Who can explain how to work out a poem's rhyming pattern?

2 Look at the second line of each verse.

   a How are they similar? How are they different?

   b Why do you think the poet has done this?

D 💬 📝 **Explore and use personification.**

Language focus

When something non-human is described using the characteristics of a person, this is called **personification**.

Example: *Ducks love to meet for daily chats about the weather.*

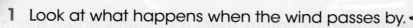

1 Look at what happens when the wind passes by.
   a How do the leaves behave?
   b What do the trees do?
   c If the wind were a person, what sort of person
      do you imagine it would be?
2 What is the poet saying about the wind?
3 Think of other ways to describe the wind using
   personification and give reasons.

   Example: *The playful wind tugs at my skirt.*

> I wonder if the 'person' would be male or female?

mischievous   angry   forgetful   excited

2 Read and compare

A 🗨 📝 **Poets use figurative
language to compare things.**

1 How would you compare
   the following things?
   Match them up and
   talk about why you chose
   a particular image.

the moon	a friend
winter	a giant breath
the sun	a night guard
clouds	restless traveller
wind	a tired old man

2 Write a simile for each one
   using either *like* or *as*.
   Example: *The moon is like
   a restless traveller who is
   always on the move.*

Language focus

Figurative language is part of our everyday
speech. You probably use comparisons
more than you realise.
A common form of comparison is a **simile**.
A simile compares things by using the
words *like* or *as*.

Examples: It's **as** hot **as** an oven in here!
              It's **like** an oven in here!

3 Think of your own images for some other natural things.
Write them in your notebook.

B  **Read another nature poem by the same poet.**

1 Before you read the next poem, discuss in groups:
   a What do emeralds, rubies, sapphires,
       diamonds and opals have in common?
   b Do you know what a flint is?
   Now read the poem to find out what the poet thinks of these things.

Flint

An emerald is as green as grass,
A ruby red as blood;
A sapphire shines as blue as heaven;
A flint lies in the mud.

A diamond is a brilliant stone,
To catch the world's desire;
An opal holds a fiery spark;
But a flint holds fire.

Christina Rossetti

2 The similes in the first stanza compare the colours of the gemstones to other
objects. Complete these sentences in your notebook:
   a An emerald is compared to …
   b A ruby is compared to …
   c A sapphire is compared to …
3 Suggest other comparisons for these colours:
   a As green as …
   b As red as …
   c As blue as …
4 How would you describe flint?

C 💬 📝 **AZ** **A contrast is a comparison that shows how two things are different, not similar.**

1 How does the flint contrast with the other stones in the poem:

   a in its appearance (in the first stanza)?

   b in its usefulness (in the second stanza)?

2 Explain which stone you would rather have with you:

   a at a party

   b on a desert island.

3 Let's look at the deeper meaning of the term *holds fire*.

   a Use some of these words to describe what flint is capable of:

> energy   power   force   life   strength

   b Explain the message of the poem in your own words.

   c Do you think the message is **subtle** or obvious?

> **subtle** *a.* not obvious or easy to notice; clever in a way that does not attract attention; delicate or not strong or bright (flavour or colour)

D 💬 📝 **Compare and contrast the poems by Christina Rossetti.**

1 Are the rhyming patterns the same or different?

2 What type of figurative language is used to describe things?

3 Identify other similarities and differences between the two poems.

E 📝 **Update your reading log with the Christina Rossetti poems you have read. Would you like to read more of her poems?**

3 Understand the form of a haiku

A 📖 💬 **One of the oldest forms of poetry is the ancient, traditional Japanese haiku. The 'form' of a poem means its structure. Some poems have a set pattern and others are written in 'free verse' without any structure.**

1 To understand the form of a poem, ask yourself the questions at the top of page 47.

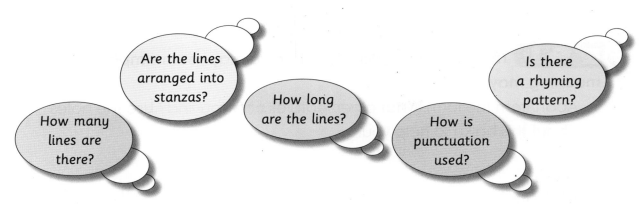

Are the lines arranged into stanzas?

How many lines are there?

How long are the lines?

How is punctuation used?

Is there a rhyming pattern?

2 Read some haiku poems. Can you work out the **form** of the haiku? Look at the number of lines and syllables.

A Bitter Morning

A bitter morning:
Sparrows sitting together
Without any necks.
James W. Hackett

Ducks upon a lake
White plumes reflect off water
Silent bobbing corks
Debbie Ridgard

Swifts shape a fly-by,
their high, riotous piercings,
and one year's shot past.
Chris Jones

Tip
Syllables are the sounds in a word. You can count the syllables by clapping the sounds as you say the word.

Example: tree (1 clap)   e/ver/green (3 claps)

bran/ches (2 claps)   de/ci/du/ous (4 claps)

Did you know?
In Japanese there are no plural words. The plural is shown by the other words in the sentence, for example *I love to write many haiku.*

B 📝 💬 👥 **The language and form of haiku may seem simple but the meaning may be deep.**

1 Apart from the form, what other features can you find? Use the notes about this haiku to help you.

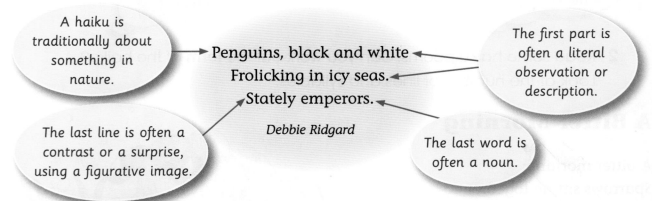

A haiku is traditionally about something in nature.

Penguins, black and white
Frolicking in icy seas.
Stately emperors.

Debbie Ridgard

The first part is often a literal observation or description.

The last line is often a contrast or a surprise, using a figurative image.

The last word is often a noun.

2 A haiku uses a few words chosen carefully for effect. With a talk partner find synonyms for these words from the poems.

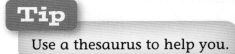

Tip

Use a thesaurus to help you.

    a plumes **b** lake **c** emperors **d** sit **e** frolic **f** piercings **g** shot

3 Haiku often show what the poet feels or thinks about something by the way the thing is described, rather than naming the emotion. Explain this in your own words.

4 In your notebook, write a list of rules for writing a haiku. Give your list an interesting title.

Doing the haiku hike!

C 📖 💬 📝 **While some traditional haiku may differ in form, most modern haiku fit the same pattern.**

1 Re-read and compare the haiku. Draw up a table and answer these questions for each one.

   a Is the haiku to do with nature?

   b Do the syllables fit the 5-7-5 pattern?

   c What literal observation or description is there in the first part?

   d What figurative image is used in the second part?

   e Identify the word at the end of the last line. Is it a noun?

   f Explain the 'surprise' or 'contrast' suggested in the last line.

> How do these poems fit the haiku hike?

Language focus

A **metaphor** compares two things directly by saying one thing is another thing.

Example: Ducks are corks!

You can change **similes** to **metaphors** by removing the words 'like' or 'as'.

Go back to the table of similes on page 44 and write each one as a metaphor.

Example: Winter is like a tired old man → Winter is a tired old man.

D 📝 **In your reading log, make a note of the haiku you have read and what you enjoyed about them.**

4 and 5 Write a haiku

A 📝 💬 **A haiku is a unique way of describing an object or a moment.**

1 In groups, think up ideas for the topic of a nature haiku.

> The sea, a tree, a seed, the sun, rain, thunder clouds, a sunset ...

2 On your own, choose a topic that means something to you. It could be something that you remember or have recently experienced, or something that has made you laugh or feel happy or sad.

3 Write your chosen topic as a heading and make two columns underneath it.

  a In column 1, write words that describe it literally and what you might see, hear, touch, taste or smell.

  b In column 2, write some figurative images (particularly metaphors) to describe it in surprising ways.

The sea	
· deep	· as deep and dark as a secret
· dark	
· hear splashing	· like a snoring giant

Tip

Write a range of different ideas, so you can use them to try out different effects.

B  **Write the first draft of your haiku.**

1 Experiment with different words from your lists to write a poem that creates the mood you want to express and that fits the haiku form.

  a Keep the first part of the haiku literal and end it with a figurative image.

  b Try to be original in how you describe the topic. Express your own feelings and thoughts.

2 Swap with a partner and give each other some useful feedback.

3 a Read through the poem.

  b Clap the syllables.

  c Give ideas for other interesting words.

Remember to do the haiku hike – 5-7-5!

4 Finalise your poem and present it for display in the classroom, adding illustrations.

How did I do?

- Did I identify and count syllables in different words?
- Did I make up literal and figurative descriptions?
- Did I plan and write a haiku?

6 Compare and perform poems

A  **Some poems have no specific structure. They are written in free verse.**

1 Listen to your teacher read a poem by Telcine Turner called *Listen*.
   Then talk about it.

   a Did you enjoy the poem?

   b What did you notice about it?

   c How did it make you feel?

Listen

Shhhhhhhhhhhhhhhhhhhhhhhhhhhhh!
Sit still, very still
And listen.
Listen to wings
Lighter than eyelashes
Stroking the air.
Know what the thin breeze
Whispers on high
To the coconut trees.
Listen and hear.

2 Read a short biography about the poet.
   Does it give any clues to why the poet
   used certain images?

Did you know?

Coconut trees are one of
the most useful plants to
humankind. They can be
used for food, fuel, oil, rope,
tools, fabrics, fertiliser and
building materials.

Telcine Turner Rolle (1944–2012) was born and grew up in the Bahamas.
She became a well-known poet, playwright and teacher. She published
a book of poems for children called *Song of the Surreys*, illustrated by
her husband. She once said: "Don't let anyone persuade you against
something you believe in your writing."

3 Re-read the poem. How would you describe its form? Compare it to
   the form of the haiku poems. What do you notice?

1 Listen to your teacher read the poem *Wind* by Dionne Brand.

2 What did you enjoy about it?

Wind

I pulled a hummingbird out of the sky one day but let it go,
I heard a song and carried it with me on my cotton streamers,
I dropped it on an ocean and lifted up a wave with my bare hands,
I made a whole canefield tremble and bend as I ran by,
I pushed a soft cloud from here to there,
I hurried a stream along a pebbled path,
I scooped up a yard of dirt and hurled it in the air,
I lifted a straw hat and sent it flying,
I broke a limb from a guava tree,
I became a breeze, bored and tired, and hovered and hung and
    rustled and lay where I could.

3 Use this checklist to **analyse** and compare the poems *Listen* and *Wind*. Write your responses in a table to show how the poems compare.

- What is the poem about?
- Who wrote it?
- Who is the 'voice' in the poem?
- How many lines and stanzas are there? Are any repeated?
- Does it have a rhyming pattern?
- Is punctuation used in any unusual ways?
- What figurative language is used?
- Does the poet's choice of words create a mood or atmosphere?
- What message or thought does the poem present?

analyse *v.* examine in detail

C **Get into small groups and decide which wind poem you enjoyed the most.**

1 a Discuss how the poem should be read aloud.

b Decide who will read which part of the poem. The whole group can read some parts (e.g. the first line) and then individuals and pairs can read other lines.

2 Practise reading the poem aloud.

3 Perform the poem to the class.

Remember to use expression and actions. Look at the audience, speak clearly, and enjoy yourself!

D **Update your reading log with the poems you have read. Do you prefer reading poems silently or aloud?**

4 Myths and legends forever

The world is full of myths and legends to explain life or inspire us with feats of heroism. In this unit, you'll explore dialogue and reported speech, understand how writers develop a screenplay and write a myth or legend of your own.

Vocabulary to learn and use:
dais, mythical, chariot, Olympus, phenomenon, hero, quest, silhouette, sovereign, epic, cartoon, screenplay, classify

1 Test your knowledge of myths and legends

A Do you enjoy tales about impossible tasks and fearless heroes? What are your favourite myths or legends?

1 Discuss the myths and legends you know.
2 List your favourite legendary heroes and mythical creatures.
3 a Do you know them from books, films or television?
   b Do you think there is any truth in the stories?
   c How do you think the stories came about?

B In fiction, the author can make any character the storyteller.

1 In small groups, skim over the extract below from a modern retelling of an Ancient Greek myth.
   a What does the narrator say he is and he is not?
   b What evidence in the story supports what he says?
   c Would you believe someone who told you this? Why?
2 Who is being welcomed in this extract?

Did you know?

Mount Olympus is the highest mountain in Greece. In Ancient Greek mythology, it was the home of the gods. Why do you think this was?

Welcome to Olympus

Well, you have opened my book. You have turned the page. You are now in ancient Greece, and you are standing on my mountain.

You had better come up.

No, I am not a ghost.

NO, I am not a giant.

I am a god. Yes, a god!

But come up higher, so we don't have to shout. I am tired of shouting.

Steep, isn't it? Too steep for most people. And the air is so thin, you may get out of breath. Take your time. I'm in no hurry.

There! You made it! Welcome! Welcome to Mount Olympus. Have you ever climbed so high? Or looked out across such vast distances? Or stood so far above the Earth?

Sit down! Choose a rock and make yourself comfortable.

And now I will tell you who I am …

I am Zeus, the great god, Zeus, the greatest of all the gods.

Zeus the all-bright, they call me.

Zeus, the bringer of light.

Yes, I am Zeus, and I rule over all other gods and goddesses.

There now, up in the sky are two of my children: Apollo wheeling the sun away till tomorrow morning, and Artemis rolling out the moon.

And the winged horse over there?

That's Pegasus.

He takes me in my **chariot** wherever I want to go. I'll tell you more about him and Apollo and Artemis later.

Jenny Koralek

chariot *n.* a vehicle with two wheels that was used in races and fights in ancient times and was pulled by a horse

C 📖 💬 **Myths and legends come from the oral storytelling tradition.**

1 Which card do you think describes a myth and which a legend?

A Stories passed from person to person based on something that once possibly happened, with heroic characters, fantastical places and unlikely events.

The plot focuses on a main character who overcomes difficulties – often a monster. Can also be about places, objects and animals.

B Stories set in the ancient past to explain the world and events that people didn't understand, such as floods, earthquakes or how the world began.

The plot often involves gods or supernatural beings and unbelievable events not based on anything factual.

2 Which titles below sound like myths and which legends?

The Yeti or Big Foot; Beowulf and Grendel; El Dorado; Thor – the God of Thunder; King Arthur and the Knights of the Round Table; How Rabbit Brought Fire to the People; Robin Hood and his Merry Men; Lost Atlantis; The Great Flood; The Loch Ness Monster.

Any volunteers
Can you retell a myth or legend from your culture or region?

3 Sort these features into two lists:
Myths and Legends.

Gods and goddesses
Heroes and villains
May be based on a historical event
Explains a natural **phenomenon**
Fantastical creatures
Set long ago
Superhuman or unlikely powers
Unlikely or exaggerated events
A classic opening e.g. *Long, long ago …*
A dangerous quest or challenge

phenomenon *n.* something unusual that exists or happens

4 Compare your list with another pair's and discuss any differences.

2 Explore the text

A Choosing who will tell the story is an important decision for a writer.

1 Think about the narrator of the extract on page 55.

   a How could you tell who the narrator is?

   b Is the extract in first person or third person narrative?

   c Find examples that show the narrator's personal views and feelings.

2 The narrator of this book tells a series of stories chapter by chapter. Thinking about who the narrator is, write a short paragraph to explain the type of stories you think the narrator will tell. Give your reasons.

3 What might an outside narrator be able to say that a character could not?

4 Find two or three parts in the extract that would change if it was an outside narrator.

   a Read the extract aloud, changing details to make it sound as if an outside narrator tells the story.

   b Make a list of things that had to change.

5 Do you prefer books written in the first or the third person? Jot down some notes and discuss your views with a talk partner. Ask each other questions to find out why.

B 💬 **Dialogue is often informal in style because it shows how the characters speak.**

1 What is your impression of Zeus from the extract?

    a List some adjectives to describe him.

    b Will he make a good storyteller for the book? Why?

2 The extract reads like dialogue but it is punctuated like narrative.

    a What features make it seem like dialogue rather than narrative?

    b Is this an enticing way to begin a book?

    c Exchange your views with another group by swapping a volunteer. Do you agree?

C 📝 **Add the extract to your reading log. Do you think you would enjoy reading more of this book?**

3 Direct and reported speech

Language focus

Direct speech directly records the actual words the characters say. When someone reports what someone else said, we call it 'reported' or 'indirect speech'.

Direct speech	Indirect speech
Zeus announced, "This is my mountain."	Zeus announced that it was his mountain.
"You are in Ancient Greece," said Zeus.	Zeus said that we were in Ancient Greece.

A 💬📝 **Discuss the differences between direct and reported speech.**

1 Use the examples above to find differences. Use these words:
    speech marks, verb tense and *that*.

2 Take turns in groups of three.

    a Privately tell one person what you did at the weekend.

    b That person tells the third person what you did.

      • Did everyone report what was said accurately?

      • Did the pronouns change? (*I* to *he* or *she*)

      • Did you use the past tense? *He or she said that …*

3 Write these sentences in your notebook in direct speech.

Example: Zeus said that he was in no hurry.

"I am in no hurry," said Zeus.

a Zeus said that they called him the greatest of the gods.

b Zeus explained that Pegasus was his winged horse.

c Zeus complained that he was tired of shouting.

Watch out for the pronouns!

B **Change direct speech into indirect speech.**

1 Write these sentences as indirect speech using correct punctuation.

Example: "I am the ruler of the gods," said Zeus.

Zeus said that he was the ruler of the gods.

a Zeus said, "I am a god.'"

b "No," confirmed Zeus, "I am not a ghost."

c "Pegasus pulls my chariot," Zeus explained.

2 With a partner, invent a dialogue between Zeus and one of his listeners. Write it out in indirect speech.

4 Test your knowledge

A *The Cat who Came Indoors is a story from Zimbabwe.*

1 Before reading the story, imagine how wild cats became domesticated.

2 In a group:

a predict the main idea of the story

b explain whether it sounds like a myth or a legend.

B **Myths and legends can be classified by their key features.**

1 Read the story on page 60 as a group to check your predictions.

a Note any features of myths or legends.

b Decide if the story is a myth or a legend, using examples from the story.

Do you think it's a myth or a legend?

2 How is this story similar to or different from a fable?

3 Are the events in this story likely? Why?

4 Do good stories have to be true to life? Give examples from a range of stories that you know.

classify *n.* to sort people or things into groups by their type

The Cat who Came Indoors

Once upon a time, there was a cat, a wild cat, who lived all by herself out in the bush. After a while she got tired of living alone and took herself a husband, another wild cat who thought she was the finest creature in all the jungle.

One day, as they strolled together along the path through the tall grass, *swish*, out of the grass jumped Leopard, and Cat's husband was bowled over, all fur and claws, into the dust.

"O-oh!" said Cat. "I see my husband is covered in dust and is not the finest creature in the jungle. It is Leopard." So Cat went to live with Leopard.

They lived very happily together until one day, as they were hunting in the bush, suddenly – *whoosh* – out of the shadows leapt Lion, right onto Leopard's back and ate him all up.

"O-o-oh!" said Cat. "I see Leopard is not the finest creature in all the jungle. It is Lion."

So Cat went to live with Lion.

They lived together very happily until one day, as they were stalking through the forest, a large shape loomed overhead, and – *fu-chu* – Elephant put one foot on top of Lion and squashed him flat.

"O-o-o-oh!" said Cat. "I see Lion is not the finest creature in all the jungle. It is Elephant."

So Cat went to live with Elephant. She climbed up onto his back and sat purring on his neck, right between his two ears.

They lived together very happily until one day, as they were moving through the tall reeds down by the river – *pa-wa!* – there was a loud bang, and Elephant sank down onto the ground.

Cat looked around and all she could see was a small man with a gun.

"O-o-o-o-oh!" said Cat. "I see Elephant is not the finest creature in all the jungle. It is Man."

So Cat walked after Man all the way to his home, and jumped up onto the thatch of his hut.

"At last," said Cat, "I have found the finest creature in all the jungle."

She lived up in the thatch hut very happily and began to catch the mice and the rats which lived in the village. Until one day, as she sat on the roof warming herself in the sun, she heard a noise from inside the hut. The voices of Man and his wife grew louder and louder until – *wara-wara-wara … yo-we!* – out came Man,

tumbling head over heels into the dust.

"Aha!" said Cat. "Now I do know who is truly the finest creature in all the jungle. It is *Woman*."

Cat came down from the thatch, went inside the hut and sat by the fire.

And that's where she's been ever since.

Retold by Hugh Tracey

How did I do?

- Did I recognise the key features of myths and legends?
- Could I tell if a story is a myth or a legend?

5 Work with words

A **AZ** **Most nouns are *countable*, which means they can be singular or plural. The plural form of most nouns is formed by adding s: *cat – cats*. Other nouns form the plural in different ways.**

1 If the word ends in **ch**, **sh**, **ss** or **x**, add **es** to form the plural. Write some sentences using these nouns in their plural form: *fox, glass, box, wish, match.*

2 If the words end in **o**, add **s** or **es** to form the plural.

a If the final **o** comes after a consonant, add **es**. Write these words and their plural forms in your notebook: *hero, echo, tornado, volcano.*

b If the final **o** comes after a vowel, add **s**. Write these words and their plural forms in your notebook: *curio, kangaroo, zoo, cockatoo.*

> That rule is easy to remember because it makes the plural words easier to say.

> Psst! Some **o** words just add **s**: **zero, kilo, piano, solo.** If you forget, use your dictionary or spellchecker.

3 When nouns end in **f** or **fe**, change the **f** or **fe** to **v** and add **es** to form the plural: *hoof* → *hooves*

   a Write these words and their plural forms in your notebook.

      leaf, life, knife, wife, elf, shelf, loaf, calf, wolf, self

B 📖 👥 **This storyteller uses various techniques to bring the story to life.**

1 Find the cat's exclamations.

   a How you can tell they are exclamations?

   b What is the effect of changing the exclamation *O-oh!* to *O-o-o-o-oh!* by the end of the story?

2 Why do you think some words are in italics? How do they help?

3 Practise saying the invented words aloud. What do they create?

4 Re-read the story in your group, making it as much fun as you can.

- Emphasise the repetition for effect.
- Use choral speaking.
- Use expression and body language.

> Remember that these stories were told long before they were ever written down.

Did you know?

Repetition helps the audience to anticipate what is coming next.

6 Who is a hero?

A 💬 📝 **What makes a hero? Work with a partner.**

1 Look up *hero* in the dictionary.

   a Discuss the different meanings.

   b Which type of hero is most likely to appear in a myth or legend?

2 What does a hero look like? Can you tell from appearance?

3 Discuss what makes a hero.

4 Draw a mind map to record a hero's qualities. Choose four qualities from the box and add names of people who might be heroes of each kind.

5 Think of and add some more qualities and names.

A famous sports person	A superhero	Someone who saves lives	A role model
Dedicates their life to helping others	Someone brave or daring	Someone with exceptional strength	A celebrity

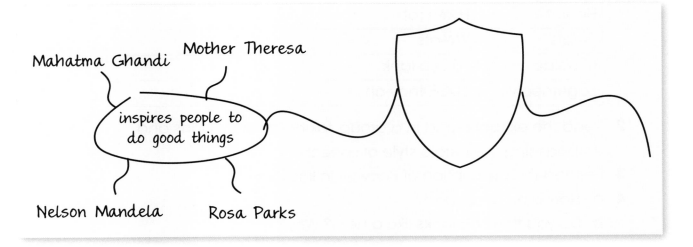

6 What might an *unsung hero* be? Suggest people you think might be *unsung heroes*.

B 📝 💬 **Who is *your* personal hero?**

1 Write a paragraph about someone you think is a hero.
   a Start with a topic sentence summarising why you chose them.
   b Justify your view with evidence in the next few sentences.
   c Describe your hero using figurative language – compare your hero to something unusual.
   d End by saying how your hero is a role model.

2 Swap your paragraph with a talk partner to find out about each other's heroes. Ask questions and make suggestions.

3 Use your partner's comments to improve your paragraph.

4 Write out your profile next to a picture of your hero for a 'heroic' wall display.

7 Meet a hero of old

(A) 📖 👥 **Beowulf is the hero of an Old English poem full of adventures and heroic deeds.**

1 Before reading the extract from a modern retelling, try pronouncing the unfamiliar names. Put the stress on the capitalised syllable.

Beowulf	BAY-oh-wolf
Hrothgar	HROTH-gar – try to join the *h* sound into *roth*
Heorot	HAY-e-rot
Geats	YAY-ats
Hygelac	HEE-ya-lahk
Edgetheow	EDGE-thay-oh

2 Read the extract aloud in a group, taking different parts and emphasising the heroic style of speech.

3 Re-read the description of Beowulf in lines 9 to 16.

4 **a** How is he described?

   b Do you think he looks like a hero? Why?

Beowulf arrives

Sometimes, King Hrothgar would return alone to his beloved Heorot. He would sit on his raised **dais**, drawing patterns in the dust with one finger. Then he would search with his eyes to see memories of firelight in the darkness and strain with his ears to hear echoes of laughter in the silence. He was an old man now. Twelve whole winters
⁵ had passed since Grendel had come to plague him.

It was at Heorot that he met Beowulf.

He was sitting in his chair, muttering to himself, when the door of the banqueting hall crashed open. He squinted as bright sunlight flooded in, capturing a million motes of dust within its golden beams. A figure stepped forward, silhouetted against
¹⁰ the light which could almost have been emanating from his own body. The dust formed a shimmering aura around him. The King trembled. Never had he seen a warrior so tall, so strong.

The stranger approached and fell onto one knee. He was dressed in a blue cloak over a silvery mail-shirt. In one hand he carried a richly decorated shield, in the other

¹⁵ a spear. His helmet masked his face but it could not hide the fair hair that tumbled down onto his shoulders nor the bright blue eyes that shone despite the shadows.

"Your majesty!" the figure said.

"Who are you?" Hrothgar demanded, recovering himself.

"My name is Beowulf," the warrior replied. "I come from the **land of the Geats**.
²⁰ I have crossed a great sea to come before you, to serve you. And I do not come alone."

There was a movement at the door and fourteen more men entered the hall, bringing with them – or so it seemed to the old king – the light that had for so long been absent. As one they knelt before him, forming a semi-circle around his throne.

"We are soldiers of King Hygelac," Beowulf continued. "My noble father was
²⁵ Edgetheow, a famous fighter among the Geats, I too have found fame in my lifetime, and seek to add to that fame by destroying the beast that has emptied this most stately hall. My **sovereign**, ever a friend of the Danes, bids me wish all health to your majesty. He too will be glad to see this monster die."

"Noble Beowulf!" the king replied. "Well is your name known to me – and that of
³⁰ your father. I bid you welcome. But this creature has already taken ninety of my finest warriors. I fear your quest is hopeless."

"Not so!" Beowulf said with a grim smile. "Tonight, as we feast once again in great Heorot, I will tell you something of my past exploits which will remove your fears for the present."

Retold by Anthony Horowitz

dais *n.* (pronounced *day-iss*) a small platform to raise someone up in a meeting hall
land of the Geats *n.* the country now known as Sweden
sovereign *n.* king

B 💬 📝 **Discuss how the author portrays Beowulf.**

1 Discuss whether you think Beowulf's looks and behaviour made him seem heroic to the king. Would it be the same today?

2 What is a *grim smile*? When might you smile in this way? Does it make Beowulf seem more or less heroic? Practise giving each other a grim smile.

3 Is the tale of Beowulf a myth or a legend? Write a paragraph to summarise your views.

    a Begin with a topic sentence that states your opinion:
       The story of Beowulf can be called ...

    b Outline the features that you identified, with examples.

    c End by using the connective *Therefore* ... to restate your opinion.

Did you know?

The ancient Norse, Danes and Swedes had many legendary heroes and mythological gods. Leif Eriksson, the most famous Viking warrior, discovered America 500 years before Christopher Columbus. Several days of the week are named after Norse gods. Do you know which ones?

C 📝 **Add *Beowulf* to your reading log. Did you find it interesting?**

8 Develop your language skills

A 📝 **Let's look at how sentences work.**

1 Are the subjects in these sentences singular or plural?

    a Beowulf kneels in front of the king.

    b Beowulf and his warriors have come to kill Grendel.

    c I knew your father well.

2 Which form of the verb *to be* is correct in each sentence?

    a I *am/are* sure that is a myth!

    b Hrothgar *is/are* the king of the Danes.

    c The Danes *was/were* massacred by Grendel.

    d Either Grendel or Beowulf *is/are* the winner of the battle.

    e Neither the people nor warriors *was/were* as brave as Beowulf.

Language focus

Sentence subjects and verbs

- The subject of a sentence means who or what is *being, having* or *doing* the action.
- The verb must 'agree' with the subject: if the subject is singular, so is the verb; if the subject is plural, so is the verb.

Singular subjects	Plural subjects
I you he/she/it	we you (can be singular or plural, depending on context) they

Example: *Beowulf challenges Grendel.*

(singular subject = Beowulf = he)

Beowulf and his warriors challenge Grendel.

(plural subject = Beowulf and his warriors = they)

Either/or and **neither/nor** can be tricky!

Either/or is singular: <u>Either</u> Beowulf <u>or</u> Grendel **is** stronger.

(= Either <u>Beowulf is stronger</u> or <u>Grendel is stronger.</u>)

Neither/nor is plural: <u>Neither</u> the Geats <u>nor</u> the Danes **are** real.

(= <u>The Geats and the Danes</u> **are** not real.)

B ✎ **Writers use different sentence types for different purposes.**

- Statements give facts or information: *Grendel is a monster.*
- Questions need an answer: *What do you want?*
- Commands give orders or instructions: *Kneel before the king.*

1   Identify these sentence types. How do you know?

   a   Why have you travelled so far to come to Heorot?

   b   Hrothgar was King of the Danes who had been massacred.

   c   Stop delaying and give me my sword.

2   Find an example of each sentence type in the extract.

3   Invent at least one sentence of each type using the word *Beowulf*.

4   Where and why are exclamation marks used in the extract?

9 Developing a viewpoint

A 💬 **Writers don't always tell you everything directly; sometimes they show you instead.**

1 Which details show that Beowulf is a hero?

2 Choose a modern-day hero and show what they are like.

    a Describe what they do and say.

    b Describe how people respond to them.

    c Use an interesting comparison to show what they are like.

3 Using Beowulf and a modern-day hero as examples, discuss whether modern-day heroes are different from ancient heroes.

4 Send a spokesperson from your group to summarise your views to another group and report back their ideas.

B 💬👥 **The characters in the extract have an unusual style of speaking.**

1 What expression shows how long it is since Grendel last attacked?

2 In pairs, read the dialogue.

    a How does Beowulf introduce himself?

    b How does Hrothgar respond?

    c Re-read the king's words in lines 29–31. How would you say the same thing?

3 Find two more examples of language you would not use today.

4 How would you describe the style of speaking? Choose evidence from the text to back up your opinion.

> formal, old-fashioned, polite, respectful, informal, impolite, unusual, hard to understand, modern, descriptive

5 With a talk partner, role play a scene where you introduce yourself to King Hrothgar, speaking in the style of the extract. Include your real name, family and where you are from.

How did I do?

- Did I greet the king respectfully?
- Did I explain my origins?
- Did I speak in heroic style like Beowulf?

10 Build a short screenplay

A 💬 📝 We understand characters in books from the narrative and dialogue. In films, we find out about them from how they act, move and speak.

1 Have you ever seen a film based on a story you have read?
   a Were the film characters the same as you imagined them from the book? Explain.
   b Was the plot the same? Was anything added in or left out?
   c Which version did you prefer? Why?
2 Which picture is most similar to how the extract describes Beowulf? Do any match your idea of him?

B 📖 💬 Cartoon strips use speech bubbles and pictures to tell the story.

1 How do you know whether a cartoon character is thinking or speaking?
2 What other visual effects give out information?
3 How does the king feel in the final frame? How would you show if he was angry?

C 📖 💬 📝 Film scripts are often planned using storyboards to work out where the actors will stand and move. The final film script includes some of this information as instructions for the actors.

1 Read this film script which is based on the cartoon sequence.

> *(Hrothgar sits alone in the hall, thinking aloud and tracing in the dust.)*
>
> HROTHGAR: **I wish the sounds of friends of old were once more all about me.**
> *(The door opens with a thud and metal clangs as Beowulf enters – framed in the doorway. Hrothgar looks up in shock)*
>
> BEOWULF: *(Kneels before Hrothgar)* **Your Majesty!**
> *(Hrothgar stares as warriors file in noisily after Beowulf)*
>
> WARRIORS: *(Bowing heads and speaking as one)* **Sire!**

2 How is this script similar to the cartoon strip?

3 Explain to each other how the film script works.

4 Using film script conventions, write the next part of the script.

5 Test your script by reading it out in your group, then improve the instructions and words.

11 and 12 Write your own myth or legend to tell

A 💬 Anyone who retells a myth or legend can bring something new to the story. Compare the myths and legends you know with the fact files below.

Myths fact file	Legends fact file
• Classic opening	• Classic opening
• Set in the ancient past	• Set long ago
• Explains a natural phenomenon	• Loosely based on historical events
• No basis in fact	• A main hero or heroine
• Gods and fantastical or supernatural beings	• Gods, monsters or powerful enemies
• Characters portraying nature (e.g. wind, rain)	• A seemingly impossible quest
• Unlikely events.	• Unlikely events.

B 📝 💬 **Retell a myth or legend you already know or invent one of your own.**

1 Use a diagram to plan your outline.

Myths	Legends
• What is the natural event?	• Who is the hero?
• Who are the characters?	• What is the task or challenge?
• How will the plot explain the event?	• How does she or he succeed?

2 Decide which details or conventions to change.

3 Write your first draft.

- Decide on a *first person* or *third person* narrator.
- Use a mixture of *direct* and *reported speech* and make the dialogue interesting and suitable for the characters.
- Add sound effects, exclamations and repetition.
- Use a variety of sentence types.

You could make the hero into a heroine, or have a different challenge – Sir Duck to the rescue!

4 Read your draft to a talk partner and listen to their feedback.

- Is the story clearly a myth or a legend?
- Are the key features clear?
- Is it lively and interesting?

5 Make corrections and improvements. Check for:

- formal English in narrative sections.
- subject–verb agreement and punctuation of direct speech.

C 👤 **Storytelling is a skill that improves with practice.**

1 Practise telling your story using expression to add drama.

Tip

Make notes in your story to remind you where and how to add emphasis and special effects.

2 Hold a storytelling event and enjoy telling and hearing each other's stories.

5 Tell me how ...

Minerals are part of our lives. Some are common to us but others are a mystery! In this unit, you'll read about the uses of salt, find out how to grow your own crystals, write instructions and learn about some amazing giant crystals deep underground.

Vocabulary to learn and use:
valuable, non-toxic, sequence, process, explanation, crystals, temperature, extreme, saturate, insulated, immense, scientists, subordinate

1 Share your knowledge about salt

A Listen to your teacher read a story. Then discuss the questions.

The Salt Princess

Once upon a time in a kingdom far away there lived a king and his three daughters. One day, eager to know who loved him the most, the king asked them, "How much do you love me?"

The eldest replied, "I love you more than gold!" The king was delighted.

The second daughter replied, "I love you more than diamonds!" The king was elated.

The youngest replied, "I love you more than salt!" The king was furious. More than salt? How dare she compare her love with something of such low value? In his rage, he banished her from the kingdom. She left, taking with her all the salt in the land.

Soon afterwards, the king's appetite began to **wane**, for the food no longer tasted good. Without nourishment, he became weak and ill, but nothing could tempt him to eat. He could no longer take pleasure in either his food or his life. As he lay dying, his youngest daughter returned, bringing a dish of warm, salty **broth**. With the first delicious taste, the king felt his strength and his relish for life begin to return.
He realised at last that his youngest daughter loved him most of all, for when she had said she loved him more than salt, she meant she loved him more than that which sustains life, and more than the joy of life itself. And that is a great love indeed.

Adapted from *More Than Salt (A Fairy Tale) by Kyddryn*
and rewritten by *Debbie Ridgard*

wane v. reduce or shrink as the Moon appears to do
broth n. thin, watery soup

1 Retell the story to your talk partner in your own words.

2 How did the king react when his daughter compared her love to salt? Why?

3 How do you think you would have reacted?

4 Why did the king become so ill?

5 How did he get better?

6 What did he realise at the end?

7 Is this story real? How can you tell?

8 What facts are there in the story about table salt?

B 📖 ✍ **AZ** **Common table salt has a history of interesting uses.**

1 Read these facts about how salt is used. Do any of them surprise you?

Did you know?

Not all types of salt are edible. Table salt is made from sodium and chloride. It's widespread on Earth and has also been found on Mars!

Salt fact file

- About 1000 years ago, some traders valued table salt as highly as gold.
- Roman soldiers were paid an allowance called a salarium to buy table salt.
- Table salt can preserve food for long periods.
- Table salt can soothe a bee sting.
- Table salt can smother a grease fire in the kitchen.
- Table salt can remove a food stain if it is rubbed onto the fabric and soaked before washing.
- Table salt helps to melt ice. A mixture of salt and grit is spread on icy roads to make them safer.

2 Do you know of any other uses for salt? Share them with the class.

3 Copy this table into your notebook and complete the first two columns. Fill in the third column as you discover new information.

Record any reference books you use in your reading log.

Salt		
What I already know:	What I would like to know:	What I have found out:

C 📖 💬 📝 **For centuries, salt was difficult to obtain and extremely valuable. Even though it is now easy to obtain, we still use many expressions associated with its value in the past.**

1   Link each expression to its meaning in your head and then use each expression in a sentence to show its meaning.

2   Work in groups to research the origins of these expressions. Use the internet, visit the library or ask an adult to help you find out more.

to take something with a pinch of salt	hard-working and valuable
worth one's salt	to realise that something you hear might have been exaggerated
to rub salt into a wound	to return to work
the salt of the Earth	a very dependable person
to go back to the salt mines	to make someone feel worse

2 Learn about style

A 📖 💬 **Style is the way a text is written. The style of a text can be personal or impersonal, depending on the purpose.**

A personal style:	An impersonal style:
Sounds friendly and relaxed	Uses formal language
Uses contractions (*I've, it's*)	Uses specialised vocabulary
Uses colloquial language	Avoids slang or contractions
Uses informal expressions	Uses second and third person pronouns (*you, it, they*)
Uses first person pronouns (*I, me, mine*)	
Can include dialogue.	Can include quotations.

1   Which of these text types are personal and which are impersonal?

3rd July   *Dear diary …*

Ingredients:
2 eggs
100g icing sugar

Having a great time. Wish you were here!

Want to meet?

Yes! Saturday OK?

a recipe   a text message from a friend   a personal diary   directions
a science experiment   a bus timetable   a postcard

2 Can you think of any texts that use a mixture of styles?

3 Would you describe the style of *The Salt Princess* as personal, impersonal or both? Give examples.

4 Compare the style of the story with the style of the *Salt fact file*. Discuss and list the differences.

B 💬 📝 **Third person pronouns are often used in impersonal texts.**

1 Explain to your talk partner what a pronoun is. Use your own words.

Language focus

You can use pronouns to avoid using the same noun over and over again.
When you write in the third person you use the third person pronouns:
he, him, she, her, it, they, them.
A pronoun can replace the subject or the object.
Example: She helps others. Others don't help **her**.

2 Replace the underlined subject or object in each sentence with the pronoun *it* or *they*.
   Example: Salt is used to flavour food and also to preserve <u>food</u>.
          Salt is used to flavour food and also to preserve <u>it</u>.
   a Everyone uses salt because <u>salt</u> is so useful.
   b There are many different types of salt but <u>these different types of salt</u> are not all edible.
   c Table salt is also known as sodium chloride and <u>sodium chloride</u> is edible.
   d Sea salt and table salt are both edible but <u>sea salt and table salt</u> are produced differently.
   e Early traders traded salt and <u>early traders</u> travelled far to find it.

3 Identify the third person pronouns in the *Salt fact file*. What noun is replaced in each case?

How did I do?

- Did I understand and use figurative expressions about salt?
- Did I identify personal and impersonal writing styles?
- Did I use third person pronouns?

A 📖 💬 **Instructions tell you what to do step-by-step.**

1 Skim the text below. What features show it is a set of instructions?
2 Read the instructions carefully. Do they make sense? Why?
3 Recall and repeat the instructions to your talk partner in your own words.

Grow a salt crystal garden

You can easily grow these **non-toxic** salt and vinegar crystals in rainbow colours.

Materials
200 ml hot water
60–80 g table salt
2 teaspoons vinegar
food colouring (optional)
a jug for mixing
a piece of sponge (or cardboard shape)
a shallow dish

Instructions
Get an adult to help you when you work with hot water.

1 In the jug, dissolve salt in the hot water and vinegar until no more salt will dissolve.
2 Place the sponge in a shallow dish.
3 Pour the salt and vinegar **solution** over the sponge until it is soaked and the liquid just covers the bottom of the dish.
4 Save the rest of the solution in a sealed jar so you can top up your growing crystals later on.
5 Dot the sponge with food colouring to add colour to the crystals.
6 Set the dish in a warm, sunny spot with good air circulation. You will see crystal growth within a day.
7 Add more solution to the dish to replace the liquid that evaporates.
8 Grow your crystals for as long as you like or until the solution is finished.

> **non-toxic** *adj.* not poisonous
> **solution** *n.* a liquid with something dissolved in it

B 📝 💬 **Instructions make the sequence clear to the reader.**

1 Why is the order of the instructions important? Are the numbers essential?
2 In your notebook, draw a simple diagram for each step, but in any order!
3 Ask your partner to number the diagrams to put them in order.

C 💬 **Share your ideas. Give your talk partner instructions on how to play a game, draw something, or go somewhere. Order your instructions correctly.**

> To cook a fish, fry it in a pan. Well, you need to catch it first!

4 Be clear and precise

A 📖 📝 **You can identify instructional language by the way the subject and the verb are arranged in the sentence.**

Language focus

A simple sentence contains a **verb** and a **subject** – the person or thing doing the action.

Example: <u>The children</u> <u>make</u> salt and vinegar crystals.
　　　　　　　　|　　　　　　|
　　　　　　subject　　verb

Instructions look as if there is no subject because the subject word *you* is not always included, only implied: (you) <u>Close</u> the door.
　　　　　　　　　　　　　　|　　　|
　　　　　(implied subject)　verb

1 Identify the verb and the implied subject in each step of the salt crystal garden instructions on page 76.

Example: (you) *Place the sponge in a shallow dish.*

2 The verbs at the beginning of each instruction are called 'command verbs'. Can you explain why?

3 Change the following sentences into instructions by removing the subject and starting with a command verb.

Example: You will answer all the questions. *Answer all the questions.*

   a The children should listen carefully.

   b Everyone will work in groups today.

   c You must follow my example.

   d Please can you open the door?

B 📖 💬 📝 **A preposition can change the meaning of a sentence.**

> A good way to remember prepositions is to think of all the places a duck can go – *into, on, up, under, over, across, against, next to!*

Language focus

Prepositions tell you where things are in relation to each other.

- A preposition is always followed by a noun, a proper noun or a *noun phrase*.
  Example: *Place the bowl <u>on</u> a flat, even surface.*
- A preposition and a noun phrase form a prepositional phrase.

1 Find the prepositions and prepositional phrases in the salt crystals instructions.

2 What happens when the preposition changes in this sentence?

Pour water | **in** / **over** / **behind** / **under** | the bowl.

Did you know?

The words *of, to* and *in* are three of the ten most frequently used words in English! What do you think the other most common words are?

3 In your notebook rewrite each sentence using the correct preposition. Draw a picture to show the correct meaning.

    a Place a sponge (*on/in/beside/under*) the dish.

    b Pour a cup of hot water (*into/over/on/around*) the jug.

    c Place the dish (*in/above/on/under*) a window ledge.

    d Throw the left-over solution (*into/down/onto/below*) the drain.

5 Write instructions

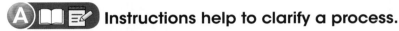 **Instructions help to clarify a process.**

1 Skim through the following texts.

2 Plan and write a set of step-by-step instructions for one of the texts.

- Refer to the salt crystal garden instructions to help you.
- Write in an impersonal style.
- Start each instruction with a command verb.

Get salt out of salty water

Salty water is put into an evaporating basin (or any shallow dish such as a saucer). It is left in a warm place and the water evaporates leaving behind the salt crystals.
We see the salt crystals starting to form at the edge of the salty water but eventually all the water will go, leaving behind just the salt.

Make a picture with salt

You could draw or trace a picture or pattern with craft glue onto white, coloured or black paper, then sprinkle salt over the glue. You need to let it dry before shaking off the excess salt. If you dab watercolour paint onto the salt, you will see the colours run along the salty glue mixture.

3 Check that your instructions include:

- headings
- a list of materials and/or equipment
- ordered steps
- specialised vocabulary
- a command verb at the start of each step
- correct prepositions
- diagrams if appropriate.

4 Ask your partner to check your work. Give each other constructive feedback.

How did I do?

- Did I write a set of instructions in order?
- Did I use command verbs?

6 and 7 Find out more

A 📖 💬 **An explanation describes how something works or happens.**

1 On page 81 there is an explanation text about the discovery of giant, underground crystals!

   a Skim the text to get an overview. Look at the headings, the topic sentences and pictures.

   b What questions do you have about this topic?

How do the features of explanations and instructions differ?

Tip

Remember, a topic sentence sums up what the paragraph is about. It's often the first sentence, but not always.

B 📖 💬 **Read the text for meaning.**

1 Find these words in the text and work out their meanings:

   a extreme **b** diameter **c** saturated **d** insulated **e** immense

2 When and how was the Giant Crystal Cave discovered?

3 What is unique about this cave?

4 Why is it closed to the public?

5 Would you like to visit the Giant Crystal Cave? Give three reasons.

6 What do the names tell you about each cave?

Can you think of other names to describe each of the caves?

The Giant Crystal Cave

What is the Giant Crystal Cave?

The Giant Crystal Cave is an underground cave containing the largest **selenite** crystals ever found. Until recently, nobody knew it existed. The cave is the size of a football field and as high as a two-storey building. Some of the crystals are over 11 m long, 4 m in diameter and weigh about 50 000 kg. Since the extreme heat and humidity in the cave are potentially lethal, it is closed to the public.

How was it discovered?

The cave was discovered in the year 2000 by miners. They were pumping water out of a mine when they stumbled upon this natural cave 300 m underground. The crystals **deteriorate** in air so scientists are working on ways to preserve them.

Where is the cave?

The Giant Crystal Cave is one of a cluster of natural cavities in the limestone rock near the Naica silver mine in the Chihuahua Desert, Mexico.

The chamber: located below the Giant Crystal Cave. It contains hot magma which heats the water in the Giant Crystal Cave.

The Cave of Swords: discovered in 1910, located 120 m above the Giant Crystal Cave. The cave is 70 m in diameter and has crystals up to 2 m in length.

The Queen's Eye Cave: discovered in 2000 at a depth of 300 m. The narrow opening of the cave resembles an eye.

The Candles Cave: discovered in 2000 at a depth of 300 m. The crystals have long, delicate structures.

The Ice Palace: 150 m below the surface, has smaller crystals and is not flooded with water.

How did the crystals form?

> Initially hot magma heated the ground water in a chamber below the cave.

> The hot water became saturated with minerals including large quantities of gypsum.

> The cave filled up with this mineral-rich hot water.

> It remained filled for about 500 000 years at a constant temperature of over 50° C (122° F).

> Eventually, these conditions allowed the crystals to grow to immense sizes.

Conditions inside the cave

It is extremely hot in the cave, around 58° C (136° F) – hot enough to cook an egg. A person can survive for about 10 minutes without protective clothing and for 45 minutes with an insulated suit and cold breathing system. The crystals are extremely dangerous because they are sharp and slippery.

selenite *n.* the crystallised form of the mineral gypsum, also known as 'moonstone' because of its colour, brilliance, and transparency
deteriorate *v.* to get into a worse condition

7 Complete these sentences with similes:

Example: The temperature in the cave is as hot as an oven.

a The cave is as big as …

b Some crystals are as tall as …

c The crystals look like …

Add two more of your own comparisons.

8 Draw a table in your notebook and compare the caves.

a Provide facts, where possible, for these headings.

b Use key words only.

Name	Discovered	Location	Description	What's inside?

9 Which cave has the most information and which has the least?

10 What conclusions can you draw from your comparison?

C In your reading log, note how much you enjoyed reading this non-fiction explanation and whether you would like to find out more.

8 Make notes

A The text *The Giant Crystal Cave* is organised into sections with pictures and headings.

1 Identify the headings and the topic sentences for each section.

2 Is the order of the sections important?

3 Can you suggest a different order that would still make sense?

4 How do the pictures help explain the information?

5 Compare the Giant Crystal Cave text with the salt crystal garden instructions. What similarities and differences are there?

B A diagram can help to explain something.

1 What type of diagram is used in the crystal cave text? Choose one from the examples on page 83?

2 Why is the diagram effective in the text?

3 Which kind of diagram would be best to make notes of the whole text? Why?

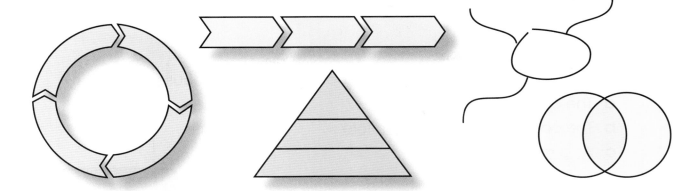

4 Use one of the diagrams to make notes of the text using key words.

5 Use your notes to give a summary to your talk partner about the Giant Crystal Cave.

6 Listen to other summaries. Which diagrams worked well to support each explanation?

How did I do?

- Did I identify how a text is organised?
- Did I use a diagram to link ideas and make notes with key words?
- Did I use a diagram to give a summary?

9 Use connectives

A 📝 💬 Sometimes the information in an explanation text is in a particular order.

Any volunteers?
Who can find five events in the text that occur in a particular order?

Language focus

Connectives link sentences and paragraphs to help a text to flow.
Time connectives sequence sentences and give clues about when an action takes place: *later, meanwhile, before, next, after, then, while, ultimately, first, eventually, recently, at length, when, initially, finally, afterwards.*
Example: <u>After</u> the cave was discovered it became famous.
Logical connectives can show cause and effect: *since, due to, because, so, therefore, thus, consequently, as a result, hence.*
Example: <u>Since</u> the cave is dangerous, you must not go inside it.

1 Identify two connectives in the text that show:

- a sequence
- a cause and effect.

2 Complete these sentences in your notebook to show cause and effect.

    a The crystals formed <u>because</u> …

    b The cave is dangerous, <u>therefore</u> …

    c <u>As a result of</u> the heat …

B 📖 📝 **Use the labelled diagram to write a short paragraph explaining how to wear the protective gear.**

How to wear the protective gear

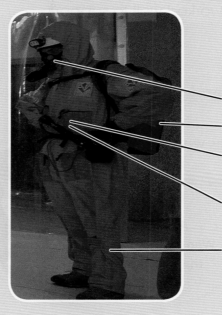

Facemask provides chilled air for breathing.

Respirator backpack (20 kg) filled with ice.

Ice vest filled with tubes of iced gel cools the body.

Insulated vest protects the skin and prevents frostbite.

Overalls keep the heat off the ice and provide protection from sharp crystals.

1 **a** Give your paragraph a heading.

    b Begin your paragraph with a topic sentence.

    c Explain how to put the gear on in the correct order.
       Use any time connectives from the word bank.

first   then   next   afterwards   finally

You can use the following example to begin your paragraph.

Wearing protective gear

In order to enter the cave you must put on protective gear.

First, put on an insulated vest to protect your skin from frostbite.

10 Working with complex sentences

Any volunteers?
Who remembers the difference between a phrase and a clause?

 A An explanation text uses sentences of different lengths. Phrases and clauses add details to make sentences more interesting and helpful.

1 Which of the following are phrases and which are clauses?

   a for many years

   b of different shapes and sizes

   c when they pumped the water out

   d inside the cave

   e while the crystals grew

   f because they deteriorate in air

   g so you must wear a suit

   h below the surface

Tip

It might help to write the examples in your notebook, then circle the subject and underline the verb.

Language focus

- A simple sentence has one clause.
- A complex sentence has one main clause with a finite verb and one or more dependent clauses.
- In complex sentences, the main clause can stand alone. The other clauses provide extra information and are introduced by subordinating conjunctions.

Example: *They stumbled upon the cave when pumping water out of the mine.*

Some subordinating conjunctions:

as   because   though   when   unless   provided   while   although   even if   as if   so that   as long as   despite

Don't forget that conjunctions are a type of connective.

2 Find the main clause in each complex sentence and write it in your notebook.

    a Giant crystals formed in the cave when it was full of hot water.

    b The cave was discovered in 2000 when miners were working nearby.

    c The crystals are dangerous because they are sharp and slippery.

    d A person will only survive for a few minutes inside the cave unless they wear protective gear.

    e If they are exposed to air, the crystals will deteriorate.

3 Use the main clauses you wrote down in your notebook to make up your own complex sentences. Add the new <u>dependent clauses</u> below.

    Example: *The crystals will deteriorate <u>unless</u> scientists can work out a way to preserve them.*

    a so they should wear protective gear

    b because the conditions were just right

    c as water was pumped out of the mine

    d although they are very beautiful

Remember, dependent clauses can go before or after the main clause.

11 and 12 Write an explanation text

A 📖 💬 📝 **There is a lot you should know about the Giant Crystal Cave before you visit!**

    1 Read an account of what it is like inside the cave.

Visiting the Giant Crystal Cave

Wearing the suit, you feel like an astronaut about to go on a spacewalk. In reality, it is not all that different, considering the harsh environment. Exploring the cave was a dream come true. I've never seen such a spectacular place. It was like setting foot on a new planet. Many of the crystals were so large that I couldn't even wrap my arms around them and the terrain was so difficult to walk on that we had to be extremely cautious not to slip and fall. Doing so would get you impaled on a sharp crystal and would require a dangerous and difficult rescue.

Adapted from *The Giant Crystal Cave* by *George Kourounis*

2 Many people would love to visit the Giant Crystal Cave but are unaware of the dangers. Design a leaflet explaining what to expect, what to see and do, what the dangers are, and how to behave in the cave in order to stay alive!

  a Think up some ideas for different sections of your leaflet. Use key words only.

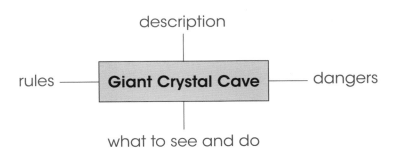

  b Use your notes to plan your paragraphs. Include:
  - a topic sentence
  - an impersonal style
  - some specialised vocabulary
  - some interesting figurative expressions and facts.

  c Include a few rules in your explanation. Use command verbs and prepositions, so your rules are clear and precise.

  d Explain what to see and do, using connectives of cause and effect to warn people of dangers in the cave.

  e Draw a diagram or picture to support your explanation of the dangers.

3 Ask someone to check your work and give you some constructive feedback.

4 Edit your work; then write it out neatly.

> **Tip**
> Use a dictionary to check your spellings.

Presentation is key. Make sure your leaflet looks appealing and is easy to understand!

6 A different type of story

Narrative poems can tell many kinds of story – old, new, mysterious, historical, funny, or just a slice of life. In this unit, you'll read three very different narrative poems. You'll compare and contrast them, develop your language to describe them and search out deeper meanings.

Vocabulary to learn and use:
internal rhyme, assonance, mystery, mysterious, theme, mood, coppice, anemone, solitude, echo, echoes, refrain, winces, gingerly, gapes

1 The Way Through the Woods

 A **Talk about a mysterious story.**

1 Summarise a mystery story you know and tell your talk partner.

2 What sort of mystery is it – an unsolved problem, a ghostly event, a detective story or something else?

 B **Read *The Way Through the Woods* by Rudyard Kipling.**

1 Skim the poem for any unfamiliar words and check how to pronounce them.

2 Now read the poem in detail. What is the mystery?

I've got goose bumps!

 **C** **Unlock the poem's secrets.**

1 a What happened 70 years ago?

b What has happened to the road now?

c Who can tell if there was once a road?

d What are the signs of a late summer evening in the woods?

e What will you hear in the woods at that time?

f What is mysterious about hearing this?

g Why do you think the road was closed?

h How do you explain the mystery?

I want to find out how the writer creates mystery and suspense so I can do it too.

The Way Through the Woods

They shut the road through the woods
Seventy years ago.
Weather and rain have undone it again,
And now you would never know
There was once a road through the woods
Before they planted the trees.
It is underneath the coppice and heath
And the thin anemones.
Only the keeper sees
That, where the ring-dove broods,
And the badgers roll at ease,
There was once a road through the woods.

Yet, if you enter the woods
Of a summer evening late,
When the night-air cools on the trout-ringed pools
Where the otter whistles his mate,
(They fear not men in the woods,
Because they see so few)
You will hear the beat of a horse's feet,
And the swish of a skirt in the dew,
Steadily cantering through
The misty solitudes,
As though they perfectly knew
The old lost road through the woods …
But there is no road through the woods.

Rudyard Kipling

2 Develop your poetic language

Language focus

Develop your poetic language

full rhyme	word ends sound the same	*flight/sight/white*
half rhyme	final sounds are similar	*bold/bald, feel/spill*
internal rhyme	words within a line have a full or half rhyme	*I am the <u>daughter</u> of Earth and <u>Water</u>*
assonance	words contain the same vowel sounds	*I h<u>ea</u>rd of a g<u>ir</u>l with a sw<u>ir</u>l in her c<u>ur</u>ls*

A  **Using words and images.**

1 With a talk partner, discuss the poem's structure using the words *stanzas* and *lines*. Why do you think the poet wrote stanzas of uneven length?

2 The poem has an unusual pattern of rhymes.

   a What is the effect of the repetition of the word *woods*?

   b Can you find a half-rhyme for *woods* in each stanza?

   c What internal rhymes can you find?

   d Can you think of another word to describe these internal rhymes?

   e Think of another word to fit each internal rhyme, matching the long, soft vowel sounds.

> Here's a clue –
> it's one of these: **assonance**,
> **simile**, **alliteration**.

B **Evocative descriptions.**

1 What is described in the first stanza?

2 What is described in the second stanza?

3 In pairs, try to work out the meaning of any unfamiliar words, then check your ideas in a dictionary or online.

C **Some words have more than one meaning so you need to use the context to identify the correct one.**

1 Which kind of **anemone** is mentioned in the poem?

> **anemone** *n.* 1. A type of small plant, wild or grown in gardens, with red, blue, or white flowers. 2. A soft, brightly coloured sea creature that looks like a flower and often lives on rocks under the water.

2   What meanings for *keeper* can you find in
    your dictionary? Which definition suits the
    context of the poem best?

3   Why do you think the keeper can tell that
    there was once a road through the woods?

4   Which are your favourite lines in the poem?
    Share them with another pair.

5   Summarise the main points of each stanza
    in one or two sentences using expressive
    words and phrases.

Anemone

Greek anemone   Snowdrop anemone
(anemone blanda)   (anemone sylvestris)

D Record the poem in your reading log, describing its mystery.

3 Something lost

A **Listen to the poem.**

1   Listen to your teacher read the poem with your eyes closed.

2   How much do you remember after listening?

3   a   Where is the story set?

    b   Who was there and what was the sequence of events?

    c   What was lost?

4   Read the poem to yourself to check your answers.

B **Analyse the mysterious effect.**

1   What poetic techniques can you identify?

2   Describe the poem's structure in terms of stanzas, lines,
    punctuation, sentences and dialogue.

   rhyme   imagery   narrative voice (who is telling the story)   language style

3   What is mysterious in the poem?

4   How did the poet achieve the mysterious effect?

Lord Neptune

1 Build me a castle,
the young boy cried,
as he tapped his father's knee.
but make it tall
and make it wide,
with a king's throne just for me.

2 *An echo drifted on the wind,*
sang deep and wild and free:
Oh you can be king of the castle
but I am lord of the sea.

3 Give me your spade,
the father cried;
let's see what we can do!
We'll make it wide
so it holds the tide,
with a fine throne just for you.

4 He dug deep down
in the firm damp sand,
for the tide was falling fast.
The moat was deep,
the ramparts high,
and the turrets tall and vast.

5 Now I am king
the young boy cried,
and this is my golden throne!
I rule the sands,
I rule the seas;
I am lord of all lands, alone!

6 The sand-king ruled
from his golden court
and it seemed the wind had died;
but at dusk his throne
sank gently down
in Neptune's rolling tide.

7 *And an echo drifted on the wind,*
sang deep and wild and free:
Oh you can be king of the castle,
but I am lord of the sea.

Judith Nicholls

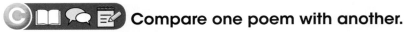 **Compare one poem with another.**

1 Practise your technique for reading a poem.

The Shell

The prettiest shell that you ever did see
I found as I played on the beach.
I laughed and I clapped my hands with glee
As it washed up within my reach.

At night when I lie in bed, my dear,
And long for the sound of the sea,
My shell I hold up to my ear.
Its music is thrilling to me.

Vilma Dubé

2 What ideas does the poem give you? Write down some notes and then exchange your thoughts with a partner. How similar or different are your ideas?

   a Who do you imagine is telling the story and to whom?

   b Why do you think they were on the beach, or long for the sea?

   c Would a different narrator change the mood of the poem?

3 Compare the structure and language of *The Shell and Lord Neptune*.

   a Talk about stanzas, lines, punctuation, sentences and dialogue.

   b Talk about poetic techniques such as rhyme, imagery, narrative voice and language style.

4 Which poem do you prefer? Why?

D **Record your reading of the two poems in your log, explaining which one you preferred and why.**

4 Read with understanding

A  Find the evidence.

1 Who narrates the main story in *Lord Neptune*?
2 Who is speaking in the second stanza? How do you know?
3 How many people speak? Give examples.
4 Write the third stanza into your notebook as a paragraph and punctuate the dialogue correctly.

B 💬 Describe the mood.

1 How do you feel when you are at the beach?
2 What is the mood of the father and son at the start of the day?
3 How does this contrast with the mood in the repeated **refrain**?
4 Choose three adjectives to describe the boy's mood in stanza five.
5 Explain the contrast in the first and second half of stanza six.
6 Who has the 'last word' that day? Will it always be the same?

The refrain sends shivers down my spine – how does it make you feel? creepy, jolly, sad, calm, peaceful, excited, mysterious, joyful?

C  Perform the poem.

1 Make notes to plan how to read the poem as a group.
   a Which parts could be read by a single voice and which as a group?
   b What sound effects or actions could add to the effect?
2 Practise reading the poem. Learn your lines by heart for added fluency. How does it sound? Does it capture the mood? Give each other feedback.
3 Perform the poem for the class.

How did I do?

- Did I capture the mood of the poem in my reading?
- Did I use performance techniques to add to the effect?
- Did I perform my part fluently and confidently?

refrain *n.* part of a song or poem that is repeated, especially between stanzas; *v.* to stop yourself from doing something

Tip

Remember, abstract nouns name things that we experience but cannot touch like ideas and feelings.

5 Not lost but found

A 📖 💬 **Read *At the End of a School Day*.**

1 How do you feel at the end of a school day? Think about the
  sounds, actions and atmosphere.

2 Summarise the end of your school day in a mind map of words
  and phrases. Use a thesaurus to help you.

3 Read *At the End of a School Day* together and compare it with
  the mood at the end of your school day.

At the End of a School Day

It is the end of a school day
and down the long drive
come bag-swinging, shouting children.
Deafened, the sky winces.
The sun gapes in surprise.
Suddenly the runners skid to a stop,
stand still and stare
at a small hedgehog
curled-up on the tarmac
like an old, frayed cricket ball.

A girl dumps her bag, tiptoes forward
and gingerly, so gingerly
carries the creature
to the safety of a shady hedge.
Then steps back, watching.
Girl, children, sky and sun
hold their breath.
There is a silence,
a moment to remember
on this warm afternoon in June.

Wes Magee

Any volunteers?
Who can say how the mood
compares to the end of your
school day?

Talk about the story.

1 Discuss the story with your talk partner.

2 **a** Why do the runners stop?

   b Why does the girl move the hedgehog?

   c What adverb says how she moves it?

   d What does this adverb mean? Use the context to help you.

   e Find two synonyms for this adverb.

3 Why do you think everyone and everything hold their breath?

4 What is the moment to remember? Summarise it in a sentence.

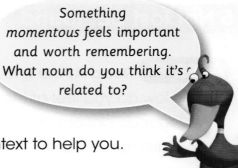

Something *momentous* feels important and worth remembering. What noun do you think it's related to?

 The poet uses figurative language, including personification.

> ## Language focus
>
> **Similes** use *like* or *as* to compare one thing to another.
> **Example:** *The children ran like the wind.*
>
> **Metaphors** say two things are the same.
> **Example:** *The final bell was music to my ears.*
>
> **Personification** is where a non-human thing is given human characteristics.
> **Example:** *The sun smiled down on us.*

1 What figure of speech is used to describe the hedgehog?

2 Make up another comparison of this type and share it with a partner.

3 Which two objects are personified in the first stanza, and how?

4 Who holds their breath in the second stanza?

   a What picture does this conjure up in your head?

   b Why is it such an effective image?

D **Narrator and tenses.**

1 Is this poem in first or third person narrative? Which words tell you?

2 How would the poem change with a different narrative person?

3 What is the tense of the poem?

4 What effect does this have on the action in the story?

E 💬 **Short and long sentences.**

1 What is the effect of sentences 2 and 3, coming after the longer first sentence?

2 What is unsettling about sentence 6? Why do you think the poet did this?

Tip

Short sentences are often simple sentences. Longer sentences are often compound or complex sentences.

Language focus

A proper sentence needs a complete verb with a subject, a number and a tense to show **who** is doing the action, **how many** there are and **when** it happens.

A **simple sentence** expresses one idea with <u>one complete verb</u> – also called a finite verb.

A **complex sentence** often expresses more than one main idea, and has **more than one** <u>complete verb</u>.

3 How many complete verbs are in sentences 4 and 5?

4 Sentences 4 and 5 have lists with commas. What is being listed?

5 Find another list with commas in the poem.

6 How many complete or finite verbs does sentence 8 have?

7 What is the purpose of the comma in sentence 8?

F 📝 **Update your reading log and record what figurative language was used.**

> Wow! I've only just realised the poem has no rhyming words – it didn't need any.

6 Use a frame to write a poem

A **Use a frame to plan.**

1 Decide on a story about finding an unusual thing in a familiar place.

2 Follow the format of *At the End of a School Day* to plan your poem.

Sentence 1	set the scene
Sentence 2	a one-line simple sentence with personification
Sentence 3	a one-line simple sentence with personification
Sentence 4	a longer sentence with three finite verbs in list format; build up to the complication with a simile
Sentence 5	a longer sentence with three finite verbs in list format; build up to the climax
Sentence 6	a simple one-line sentence emphasising the build-up
Sentence 7	a simple sentence creating the drama of the climax
Sentence 8	a simple sentence expressing a final thoughtful reflection

B **Write without stopping.**

1 Write your first draft in the present tense to create immediacy.

2 Make sure every word counts. Use a thesaurus to help you choose effective adjectives, adverbs and descriptive language.

3 Ask your talk partner to read your poem aloud. How does it sound? Does it flow and create the mood and drama that you want? Make changes to improve it.

C **Read out each other's poems.**

1 Swap and read each other's poems aloud in a group. Does your poem sound how you expected? Say what you liked about how your poem was read out, and what you enjoyed about the other poems you heard.

Hurray!
I'm a poet although
I don't know it!

How did we do?

- Did we read each other's poem with expression and feeling?
- Did my poem sound how I expected or was I able to explain what was different to how I imagined it would sound?

7 A box of delights

Traditional tales are a box of delights, from stories old and new to tales of flying carpets, tricky customers and cunning characters. You'll look at different versions of an ancient fairy tale, meet a modern hero, read about a clever princess and write your version of her story.

Vocabulary to learn and use:
traditional, culture, cultural, synopsis, synopses, flee, Persia, Iran, Cinderella, fairy tale, gourd, drama, ambiguity

1 Fairy tales forever

A  **Some fairy tales have been retold around the world for centuries.**

Today, Persia is called Iran. Do you know any other countries that have changed their names?

1   In a group, read the **synopsis** of this traditional Persian tale. What other fairy tales does it remind you of? What is similar and what is different?

Synopsis

Settareh has to do all the chores for her stepmother and wears her stepsisters' old clothes. Jealous of her beauty and good nature, they mock her rags until she feels ashamed. Meanwhile, the king invites everyone to the New Year, *No Ruz*, celebration. Instead of buying a dress, Settareh spends her money on others in need and an unusual blue jug, which turns out to be enchanted. She wishes for a beautiful gown for *No Ruz*. At the celebration, she meets a handsome prince but has to **flee** dramatically to avoid her stepmother and in so doing loses her anklet.

The prince eventually finds Settareh but her jealous sisters find the jug and wish to be rid of her. Six jewelled hairpins appear which they pin into Settareh's hair, turning her into a turtledove. Although the prince thinks he has lost her, Settareh, the bird, sings to him each evening. One night, he sees the pins, pulls them out and so sets Settareh free. They live happily ever after.

Rewritten by *Sally Burt*

> **synopsis** *n.* a short description of the contents of something such as a book or film
> **flee** *v.* to escape by running away, especially because of danger or fear

B 🗨 📝 **Compare different versions of the *Cinderella* story.**

1 Listen to your teacher read a synopsis of *Cinderella*. How does it compare with other versions that you know? If you have seen a film version, how does it compare with that?

Did you know?

The Disney film of *Cinderella* is based on a 17th century French version of the story called *The Little Glass Slipper* by Charles Perrault.

2 How many of these fairy tales do you know?

Little Red Riding Hood; The Giant Turnip;
Jack and the Beanstalk; The Pied Piper of Hamelin;
The Princess and the Pea, Stone Soup;
The Emperor's New Clothes; Pinocchio;
The Ugly Duckling; The Shoemaker and the Elves,
The Magic Pillow; The Selfish Giant;
Aladdin and the Magic Lamp.

3 Create a mind map of other fairy tales you know. Include key details.

4 Summarise one of the stories to a partner.

5 Do your stories have any similar characters, themes, events or endings?

6 Share your stories with another pair. Which key traditional tale features do they share?

Have you included traditional tales from your region?

- unlikely events
- a timeless setting (*Once upon a time*)
- enchanted objects
- wicked stepmothers
- a good nature triumphing over greed, selfishness or wickedness
- a task or test; cleverness rewarded
- three people/events/wishes/ challenges
- themes like good–evil, poor–rich, generous–selfish
- transformation, for example rags to riches, proud to humble, greedy to generous.

2 Compare and contrast

Tip

Break down unfamiliar names into syllables to help you pronounce them: *Set/tah/reh*
Yeh/Shen
Chin/ye

(A) 📖 💬 **Explore different versions of the** *Cinderella* **tale.**

1 Skim the synopses from China and Kenya. Have you heard these versions or similar versions in your region?

2 How are they similar to or different from the *Cinderella* and *Settareh* stories? Tell your partner.

Cinderella in China

Tuan Ch'eng-shih wrote the earliest known version of Cinderella in the mid 9th century.

Yeh-Shen's stepmother treats her harshly. Her only friend is a magical fish in the river. One day, her stepmother catches the fish and cooks it for supper. An old man tells the miserable Yeh-Shen to keep the fish bones and make a wish when she really needs something. When she wishes to be able to attend the Spring Festival, her clothes are transformed into an exotic outfit with golden slippers. Yeh-Shen loses one golden slipper while fleeing her stepmother at the festival. The king searches for its owner. The king's men catch Yeh-Shen creeping in to reclaim her slipper and bring her before the king. When she puts it on, her beautiful festival outfit reappears. The king falls in love with Yeh-Shen and they marry.

Rewritten by *Sally Burt*

Cinderella in Kenya

Chinye's cruel stepmother sends her into the night forest to fetch water but instead of attacking her, the animals keep her safe. On her return, Chinye meets an old woman who asks her to sweep her hut. She tells Chinye to take the tiniest, quietest gourd from the floor and break it open at home. When Chinye does so, treasure spills out of the gourd. Her greedy stepsister dashes off to find the old woman's hut but instead of sweeping the floor and taking the tiniest gourd, she grabs the largest and scurries home. Instead of treasure, a swarm of vicious wasps bursts out forcing the stepmother and stepsister to flee. Chinye is alone, but instead of spending her wealth on herself, she invites the village women to share it and build a thriving community.

Rewritten by *Sally Burt*

B 📖 📝 **Re-read all the synopses and try to answer the questions without looking back at them.**

1 **Persia**
  a How do Settareh's stepsisters make her feel ashamed?
  b What does Settareh do instead of buying a dress?
  c What does this tell you about her nature?
  d How do the sisters show they are more jealous than ever?
  e How does Settareh show her loyalty and how is it rewarded?

2 **China**
  a Who is Yeh-Shen's only friend? Why do you think this is?
  b What does Yeh-Shen wish for and how is her wish answered?
  c Why do you think Yeh-Shen's wish is granted?

3 **Kenya**
  a How can you tell that Chinye's stepmother does not care for her?
  b Why do you think the animals protect Chinye?
  c How is Chinye's life transformed in the story?
  d What does Chinye do instead of falling in love with a prince?

4 Swap books with a partner and check each other's answers.

C 📝 💬 👥 **Which key *Cinderella* elements appear in different versions of the tale?**

1 In pairs, draw up a table of key *Cinderella* features and tick which of the stories share each one.

Cinderella story element	Yeh-Shen	Chinye	Settareh
Wicked or mean stepmother	✓	✓	✓

2 Prepare a short oral report on the different versions of the story.

3 a Introduce the report explaining what it is about.

 b Explain how two or three key elements from your table differ or are similar.

 c Finish by saying which version you prefer and why.

4 Present your report to another group or another class.

> **Tip**
>
> When you give a presentation, don't write out your speech in full; just use cards with key words to remind you of the main points.

D 📝 **Add the *Cinderella* synopses to your reading log. Which one did you prefer?**

3 Verb tenses

A 📖 📝 **AZ** **Fairy stories are often set *long, long ago*, or *once upon a time*.**

1 What tense is a story usually written in?

2 What tense is used in each synopsis? What is the effect?

 a In pairs, each read one synopsis to the other, one partner changing the story into the past tense and the other into the future tense.

 b How does the tense change the effect of the story?

3 Choose the correct form of the verb *to be* to make these sentences happen right now.

 Example: Yeh-Shen (to be) is feeding her friend the fish.

 a Settareh's sisters (*to be*) teasing her again.

 b While Settareh (*to be*) singing, the prince spots the pins.

 c The animals (*to be*) protecting Chenye from harm.

 d "Why (*to be*) you crying?" asked the old man.

Language focus

The simple form of the present tense shows things that are done repeatedly. It shows it has been done before and it is likely to be done again.

Example: *We walk to school. I read before I go to sleep.*

Can you add **always**? *Then it's the simple present!*

The longer form of the present tense indicates something being done 'right now'. It has a present participle of the verb along with a 'helping' or **auxiliary** verb.

The present participle always ends with **ing**:

fishing, eating, swimming, carrying, smiling, singing

The helping verb is the verb *to be*:

am, is, are or *was, were*

The helping verb agrees with the subject but the **ing** verb stays the same.

She   is   writing   an   email.

subject   helping verb   present participle

They are listening to a story.

Can you add 'right now'?

4 Write down the underlying verb from each of the sentences in question 3 on page 103.

   Example: feeding → *feed*

5 Choose a suitable present participle to complete these sentences:

   Example: *The prince is (verb) searching for Settareh.*

   a The gourds are all (*verb*) to be picked up by Chenye.

   b Why is Yeh-Shen (*verb*) from the festival?

   c What are you (*verb*) for *No Ruz* this year?

   d We are (*verb*) the king will notice us at the festival.

B  **Helping verbs are also used to form longer versions of the past tense.**

Language focus

The longer form of the past tense shows that someone was doing something when something else happened.

Past tense of *to be*   present participle

I <u>was</u> <u>talking</u> on the telephone <u>when the doorbell rang</u>.

main clause   subordinate clause

1 Put this sentence into the past tense by changing <u>just one word</u>.
Yeh-Shen is longing to go to the festival.

2 Think of a rule for creating the longer past tense using the verb *to be* as the helping verb.

3 Discuss possible endings for these sentences.
Example: Cinderella was sitting all alone <u>when</u> her fairy godmother appeared.

> Adverbial connectives link two parts of a sentence by introducing an adverbial clause that says **when**, **where** or **how** the action happened.

  a Chenye was doing her chores <u>before</u> (*subordinate clause*).

  b The prince was listening to the songbird <u>when</u> (*subordinate clause*).

  c Yeh-Shen was weeping by the river <u>after</u> (*subordinate clause*).

4 and 5 Write a synopsis

A **The *Cinderella* story still inspires books and films today. Each new version adds fresh ideas to make it original and different.**

1 In pairs, discuss ideas for a *Cinderella* story.

  a What will the Cinderella character be like?

  b Who will the other main characters be?

  c Where will it be set? What local colour will you include (such as clothing, way of life and culture)?

  d What will be the climax and resolution?

> **Local colour** means details which are special and particular to your region.

2 Use a flow chart to plan the story with key words and phrases:

| Introduction: setting and main characters | 'Cinderella problem' | Helping hand | Climax | Resolution |

Include local colour from where you live.

3 Together, write a synopsis of the story.
- Use the present tense.
- Use the third person narrative.
- Use simple, compound and complex sentences to add interest.

4 Review and edit your synopsis to make sure it flows, covers the key elements of your story and includes some local colour.

5 Read your synopsis to another pair.
   Ask questions about each other's stories.

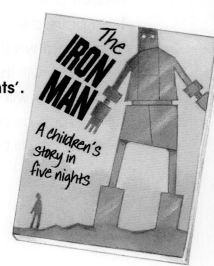

Any volunteers?
Who'd like to retell their story to the class?

How did I do?

- Did I include only the key points of the story?
- Did I write consistently in the present tense, using the third person narrative?
- Did I include local colour?

6 The Iron Man

A 📖 💬 *The Iron Man* is a short novel by Ted Hughes.
The author describes it as 'A Children's Story in Five Nights'.

1 Discuss the title of the novel.
- Who or what do you think the book will be about?
- Do you think it is based on a real character?
- What genre of book do you think it is? Why?

2 Read the chapter summaries below. Can you work out which summary belongs with each title and predict the sequence of the chapters?

Chapter titles

What's to be Done with the Iron Man?

The Coming of the Iron Man

The Iron Man's Challenge

The Space-Being and the Iron Man

The Return of the Iron Man

Chapter synopses

A The next spring, the Iron Man frees himself. Hogarth takes the Iron Man to a scrap yard full of iron to eat and befriends him.

B A black speck appears on a star, heads for Earth and lands on a large part of Australia. It is a gigantic space-bat-angel-dragon who makes war on Earth. Hogarth begs the Iron Man to help.

C Hogarth, a farmer's son, discovers an Iron Man which has been eating cars and tractors. Frightened locals lure the Iron Man into a huge pit and bury him. Only Hogarth feels sorry for the Iron Man.

D The Iron Man is taken to Australia where he challenges and defeats the space-bat-angel-dragon in a test of strength. The Iron Man orders the space-bat-angel-dragon to return to space and sing to the Earth from the sky, which causes people on Earth to live more peacefully.

E The Iron Man appears on the cliff and falls into the sea, breaking into pieces. The pieces slowly find each other as he rebuilds himself.

3 Who do you think are the main characters in the novel?

4 Your teacher will tell you the correct order of the chapters. Did you guess correctly? Discuss any surprises.

Any volunteers?
Who'd like to share their chapter order and say who the main characters are?

B 📝 💬 **Each chapter in a novel is a mini-story in itself as well as being part of the main story.**

1 Use the chapter summaries to complete a table in your notebook, showing how the plot fits with the key structure features of a story. Use evidence from the summaries or titles to explain your thinking.

Did you know?

Before books were common, novels were published in instalments in magazines. Each instalment usually ended on a climax to persuade readers to buy the next issue.

Chapter	Key story stage	Evidence from the story
Chapter 1	Introduction	The main character ...

Introduction | Build up | Problem | Resolution | Conclusion

2 Compare your table with a partner's and discuss the differences.

3 Write three paragraphs below your table.

- **Paragraph 1:** Explain who the main characters are and which details in the summaries make you think so.
- **Paragraph 2:** Give the *genre* of the book using evidence from the text.
- **Paragraph 3:** Say whether you would like to read the full novel and why.

Tip

Start each paragraph with a clear topic sentence saying what the paragraph is about.

7 The Coming of the Iron Man

A 📖 💬 📝 **The chapter titles capture our interest in the chapter.**

1 What questions does the title of Chapter 1, *The Coming of the Iron Man*, bring to mind?

2 Read the opening of Chapter 1, focusing on how drama is created by:

- the action – *what happens*
- the vocabulary and the descriptions – *exciting words and figurative language*
- the variety of sentences – *long and short sentences, questions, statements, exclamations*
- the layout and textual features – *unusual layout of lines, how words are written, repetition.*

3 Note down two examples of each method of creating drama.

4 With your partner, compare your examples, saying why you chose them.

5 Is this a dramatic opening for the novel? Discuss your opinion, using examples from the text.

The questions and answers in the second paragraph make me want to know more. Nobody knows …

The Coming of the Iron Man

The Iron Man came to the top of the cliff.

How far had he walked? Nobody knows. Where had he come from? Nobody knows. How was he made? Nobody knows.

Taller than a house, the Iron Man stood at the top of the cliff, on the very brink, in the darkness.

The wind sang through his iron fingers. His great iron head, shaped like a dustbin but as big as a bedroom, slowly turned to the right, slowly turned to the left. His iron ears turned, this way, that way. He was hearing the sea. His eyes, like headlamps, glowed white, then red, then infrared, searching the sea. Never before had the Iron Man seen the sea.

He swayed in the strong wind that pressed against his back. He swayed forward, on the brink of the high cliff.

And his right foot, his enormous iron right foot, lifted – up, out into space, and the Iron Man stepped forward, off the cliff, into nothingness.

CRRRAAAASSSSSSSH!

Down the cliff the Iron Man came toppling, head over heels.

CRASH!

CRASH!

CRASH!

From rock to rock, snag to snag, tumbling slowly. And as he crashed and crashed and crashed

His iron legs fell off.

His iron arms broke off, and the hands broke off the arms.

His great iron ears fell off and his eyes fell out.

His great iron head fell off.

All the separate pieces tumbled, scattered, crashing, bumping, clanging, down on to the rocky beach far below.

A few rocks tumbled with him.

Then

Silence.

Only the sound of the sea, chewing away at the edge of the rocky beach, where the bits and pieces of the Iron Man lay scattered far and wide, silent and unmoving.

Only one of the iron hands, lying beside an old, sand-logged washed-up seaman's boot, waved its fingers for a minute, like a crab on its back. Then it lay still.

While the stars went on wheeling through the sky and the wind went on tugging at the grass on the cliff top and the sea went on boiling and booming.

Nobody knew the Iron Man had fallen.

Ted Hughes

B 📝 💬 **Discuss the author's description of the Iron Man.**

1 Draw a picture of the Iron Man based on the description in the extract. Surround him with descriptive words and phrases from the text.
   • Include at least two similes.
   • Include words and phrases to describe his size, the way he moves and how he falls.

2 Imagine you were with Hogarth when he first saw the Iron Man. What would you think and feel? Write your reaction in a thought bubble under your picture.

C 💬 📝 *The Iron Man* **has been described as a modern fairy tale.**

1 Thinking of the features of fairy tales, use what you know about *The Iron Man* to list reasons for agreeing and disagreeing.

The Iron Man is a modern fairy tale	
Reasons for agreeing	Reasons for disagreeing
It contains a challenge.	It is not set long, long ago.

2 Do you agree that it is a modern fairy tale?

D 📝 **Add** *The Iron Man* **extract to your reading log. Would you like to read the rest of the book?**

8 Variety adds power to writing

A 📖 💬 📝 **Sentences make writing work.**

1 Find a statement and a question in *The Iron Man* extract. How did you identify them?

2 Why do you think there are no commands in this extract?

3 Why do exclamation marks appear after single words?

4 What adds to the effect of these exclaimed words?

5 a What parts of speech do these underlined phrases stand in for – adjectives or adverbs?

> <u>Taller than a house</u>, the Iron Man stood at the top of the cliff, <u>on the very brink</u>, <u>in the darkness</u>.

   b Change the words to make each underlined phrase mean the opposite.

Language focus

There are three main forms of sentence. Each sentence form can also be a **simple**, **compound** or **complex sentence**.

Sentence type	Purpose	End punctuation	Example
Statement	states facts	.	The Iron Man looked at the sea.
Question	needs an answer	?	What is it?
Command	gives an order	. or !	Do not walk close to the edge.

Exclamation marks (!) can be used with single words, phrases or full sentences. They express strong feeling or emphasis. *That is terrifying! Oh no! CRAAAASH!*

6 In pairs, find some other sentences in the extract with several descriptive phrases. Change their meaning by substituting alternative phrases or single adverbs.

7 Write a simple sentence of your own to describe a scene and extend it with descriptive phrases.

- Include at least one adjectival phrase (*describing a noun*).
- Include at least one adverbial phrase (*modifying a verb*).

Tip

Phrases are groups of words that belong together but do not contain a verb. They can do the job of adjectives, adverbs or nouns.

B **The author doesn't always write in standard or formal English.**

1 a In what ways is excerpt A of *The Iron Man* text on page 109 **not** written in standard English? Why do you think the author chose to do this?

  b How could you turn excerpt A into formal English?

2 Two of the statements in excerpt B on page 109 are simple sentences. What sort of sentences are the other two? How can you tell?

3 Look through the extract on page 109 to find:

  a phrases used instead of proper sentences

  b a new line starting in the middle of a sentence or phrase.

4 Why do you think the author uses this unusual style and layout? Do you think it is effective?

C 📖👥 **The full effect of an author's choice of words, sentences and style is sometimes only clear when you read aloud.**

1 Read the main extract aloud with a talk partner.
   • Use the variety of sentence types and lengths as well as the punctuation and layout to interpret the dramatic effect.
   • Explore creating different effects through different styles of reading, tone of voice and pace.

9 Traditional tales

A 💬👥 **Fairy tales are only one type of traditional tale. Many traditional tales share similar features. In some, cleverness is especially admired.**

1 What makes the title *Nine Questions for a Princess* sound like a traditional tale?
2 How might 'cleverness' come into this story?
3 Read the extract aloud in groups of three: one for each character and a narrator. Focus on making the dialogue lively and fun.

Princess Suryaprabha has promised to marry any man who can ask her a question she cannot answer. Each man can ask nine questions in total.

> **Tip**
>
> Pronounce the names like this:
> Suryaprabha – SUR/ya/pra/BHA
> Shashishekhar – SHA/shi/SHE/khar

B 💬 **The text on page 113 is an extract from the full story.**

1 In your group, discuss what story feature shows which part of the story it is.
2 Describe the 'cleverness' highlighted in the story?
3 Why did Suryaprabha choose this test? What did she want in a husband?
4 Share your ideas with another group. Ask and answer questions about how the story might have begun.

C 📝 **Note your opinion of *Nine Questions for a Princess* in your reading log.**

Nine Questions for a Princess

The next day, [Shashishekhar], a handsome young man appeared in court. He was dressed simply but his eyes shone bright with the light of knowledge. He announced that he had nine questions for the princess and, in no time, was sitting before her.

"How many stars are there in the sky?" was his first question.

Suryaprabha replied, "There are as many stars as there are hairs on a goat."

"Which is the most beautiful child on earth?"

"For every mother, her child is the most beautiful."

"What is the difference between truth and lies?"

"It is the difference between our eyes and ears. Our eyes will always see the truth but our ears can hear both truth and lies."

"Which person has hands, yet is considered handless?"

"A rich man who does not share his wealth."

"Who has eyes but is still blind?"

"A man without compassion, who does not see the suffering that exists in this world."

Then Shashishekhar showed her a picture of a crumbling palace and asked what it meant. By now the princess was sure this was no ordinary man. But it did not take her long to give her answer.

"A house without a proper foundation, be it a palace, will collapse."

He showed another picture – of an old lady collecting firewood, while carrying a heavy load on her back.

The princess smiled and replied, "This picture depicts human greed. The woman has collected so much wood, yet she does not want to give up and go home."

Now, the princess had answered seven questions accurately. There were only two left. Shashishekhar then asked a very clever question:

"Princess, which is the question you can't answer?"

Suryaprabha was stumped. If she told him, Shashishekhar would ask that question as the last one, and if she did not, she would lose anyway. She smiled and bowed her head. "I accept defeat."

Thus it came to be that the two wisest people in the kingdom got married and lived happily.

Sudha Murty

10 Pronouns and prepositions

A 💬 Pronouns stand in for nouns to help avoid repetition but it is important to make sure that it's clear which noun the pronoun represents.

Personal pronouns	Possessive pronouns	Possessive adjectives
I, you, he, she, it, we, they	mine, yours, his, hers, ours, theirs	my, your, his, her, its, our, their

1 In the sentence below, whose slippers are they?

> Suri asked her sister whether the slippers she was wearing were hers.

2 Explain the **ambiguity** in these sentences.

  a Jerome won't play chess with his brother because he always wins.

  b As Lily took her book out of her bag, she dropped it.

  c The bus crashed into the gate but it wasn't damaged.

3 Suggest ways to make the meanings clear.

> **ambiguity** *n.* having more than one possible meaning and possibly causing confusion

B 💬 📝 Possessive adjectives (linked to possessive pronouns) or determiners can also be ambiguous.

1 What is ambiguous about these sentences?

  a Rafael visited Amal after <u>his</u> birthday.

  b The teacher gave the student <u>her</u> pen.

  c Indira's friend and <u>her</u> mother came to tea.

> Remember, adjectives modify or describe a noun but pronouns are used in place of a noun.

2 Suggest ways to make the meanings clear.

3 Are the underlined words adjectives or pronouns?

  a I lost my coat so the prince gave me <u>his</u>.

  b We gave <u>our</u> opinion of the story.

  c The old woman bent down to pick up <u>her</u> bundle of sticks.

  d That idea was <u>mine</u>.

  e <u>Their</u> answer was that the ball was <u>theirs</u>.

Language focus

Homophones are words that sound similar but have different spellings and meanings.

their (possessive adjective)
there (adverb of place)
they're (contraction of *they are*)

4 Use *their*, *there* or *they're* to complete each sentence correctly.

  a What happened to __ shoes?

  b Do you want me to stand here or __ ?

  c If __ ready, they can begin walking.

  d I will prepare __ lunch before I go.

  e When __ ready, we can watch them perform.

  f We saw him over __ under the balcony.

11 and 12 Your own tale

A 🗨️📝 **Plan your own question and answer story based on**
Nine Questions for a Princess.

1 In groups of three, plan your tale.

Part one (mainly narrative): Introduction and build-up	Part two (mainly dialogue): The test, resolution and conclusion
Main characters?	What questions will be asked?
Issue or complication leading to test?	How will they be answered?
What is the test to prove?	Do they pass the test?
Who will tell the story?	How will the story end?

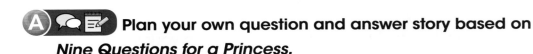

Introduction | Build up | Test | Resolution | Conclusion

  • For each part, discuss: **how, why, who, what, when, where**?

  • Invent seven new questions, with clever answers.

  • Think of an unusual ending and a title to match the story.

2 Decide who will write what and write a first draft.

Why not make the characters and setting more modern?

3 Share your drafts, give each other feedback and revise your story. Check for:

- traditional tale beginnings and endings
- different sentence types and lengths
- different sentence starters
- interesting vocabulary, adverbial and adjectival phrases, and figurative language
- different positions of phrases and clauses in longer or complex sentences
- dialogue correctly set out and punctuated
- expressive exclamations and interesting layout features.

4 Create a final version of your story. Proofread your work and add an illustration.

B 👥 **Traditional tales are for sharing!**

1 Practise reading your story aloud, emphasising the drama and cleverness in your delivery.

2 Amaze and confound another group by reading them your story!

How did I do?

- Did we read clearly and fluently as well as adding some drama?
- Did we use expression, pace and body language especially for dialogue?
- Did we read together well as a group?

8 Share your views

How do you like to relax? What do you enjoy? Would you prefer to watch a film or read a book? In this unit, you'll look at advertisements for different activities, practise being persuasive, analyse film reviews and write a letter expressing your opinion.

Vocabulary to learn and use:
appeal, font, slogan, promote, persuade, preposition, review, genre, commentary, contraction

1 Analyse a poster

A 📖 💬 **Posters are everywhere. Can you think of any or see any right now?**

1 What is a poster? What does it do?

2 Skim through this poster and identify the following features:
- eye-catching design
- large font
- key heading
- catchy slogan
- powerful words
- factual information
- a specific audience.

3 Read the poster in detail and understand more.
   a What is it promoting or advertising?
   b Who is the intended audience?
   c Where would you find a poster like this?
   d Identify any **persuasive devices** used to get people interested.

> **persuasive device** *n* a language technique used to influence the way we think or feel

---

Lori Lane Carnival

Saturday 15th August

10.00–20.00

Entrance is free!

Tickets for rides and events available at the kiosk

Fun galore and so much more!

Young or old, there's something for everyone.

**FUN!
FOOD!
PRIZES!
MUSIC!
GAMES!**

- Live entertainment
- Fabulous food stalls
- Crazy carnival games
- Giant jumping castles
- Creepy climbing wall
- Fun face-painting
- Playful puppet shows
- Happy hat competition

Proceeds will go towards upgrading the library. For more information, contact the librarians.

> Would you go to this event? What would you enjoy the most?

B 📖 💬 **Advertisements can be persuasive, informative or both.**

1 What information does the advertisement for the carnival provide?

When and where is it happening?

What's the entrance fee?

How can I get more information?

Can I bring my baby brother?

What do I need a ticket for?

2 Think of your own questions. With a talk partner, take turns to ask and answer your questions.

C 📝 💬 **Most of the information is given as key words and phrases rather than full sentences.**

1 Why do you think this is?

2 Do you think the poster would be as effective with full sentences? Why?

3 Write full sentences using the key words from the poster. Make your sentences sound as positive as possible.

Example: Delicious dishes will be available at a wide variety of food stalls.

> ## Did you know?
>
> Centuries ago, all posters were handmade. Posters only became mass-produced when printing techniques were developed in the late 1700s.

2 Sound persuasive

> Speak clearly, use expression, sound enthusiastic and use sound effects!

A 👥 **Being persuasive depends on the way you speak and the words you use. Have you ever been persuaded by someone to do something you didn't want to do? How did they persuade you?**

1 With your talk partner, take turns to role play a radio presenter advertising the carnival event.

2 How will you make sure that you are noticed and heard?

B 📖 👥 📝 **You don't have to exaggerate to be persuasive.**

Choose words that give a positive but realistic impression.

1 In each sentence below, which words sound:

   a the most positive?

   b positive but realistic?

- The carnival is open to *the whole world/young and old*.
- At the carnival you will find *everything your heart desires/something for everyone*.
- Come and have *the time of your life/loads of fun*.

2 Role play a conversation with a partner, taking turns to persuade each other to go to the carnival. Be positive but realistic.

3 Read and compare these advertisements.

Experience a pleasant holiday

Visit our family holiday hotel. The rooms are a reasonable size with comfortable beds and a shower. At meal times guests can enjoy healthy, home-cooked food.

Experience a once-in-a-lifetime holiday!

Visit our superb family hotel for the best holiday you will ever have. Our vast rooms have the world's most luxurious beds and a state-of-the-art shower fit for a king. At meal times, guests will savour the most delicious food they can ever hope to experience.

   a Which one sounds more appealing? Which one sounds more realistic? Which one would you trust?

   b Write your own advertisement for the hotel. Make it appealing but realistic. Remember to sound positive and enthusiastic but don't bend the truth.

  **Read for meaning.**

1 Skim over this poster. What is it about?

Dublin Mountaineer Bus Service

The Dublin Mountaineer bus provides transport for walkers and hikers who want to enjoy the Dublin mountains on weekends and holidays.

Sandyford Luas	1000	1130	1300	1515	1700
Enniskerry Road (Aikens Village)	1009	1139	1309	1524	1709
Ballyedmonduff Road	1018	1148	1318	1533	1718
Glencullen	1022	1152	1322	1537	1722
Wicklow Way (Bus Terminus)	1024	1154	1324	1539	1724
Tibradden	1032	1202	1332	1547	1732
Cruagh/Killakee	1036	1206	1336	1551	1736
Grange Road (Marlay Park)	1053	1223	1353	1608	1753
Sandyford Luas (Drop-off only)	1105	1235	1405	1620	1805

Tickets available on the bus: daily €5

Family rambler €12 (2 adults, 2 children)

Dublin Mountains Partnership. For more information visit **www.dublinmountains.ie**

2 What is a *mountaineer*? Look up the meaning in a dictionary.
3 a What does the name of the bus service suggest about the activity and the area the bus covers?
   b Do you think it is a good name for this bus? Why?
   c Which type of figurative language is used in the name *Dublin Mountaineer*?
4 Re-read the poster, then take turns with your talk partner to tell each other as many details as you can, without looking back at it.
5 Discuss how that went. Did you remember all the details and sound enthusiastic? Was it difficult? Why?

B 💬 📝 **What is the purpose of the**
***Dublin Mountaineer* poster?**

1 **a** What is it advertising or promoting?

b Is it persuasive, informative or both? Give examples.

c Draw a table in your notebook to compare the *Dublin Mountaineer* poster with the *Lori Lane Carnival* poster, using these headings:

Features to look out for

- · eye-catching design
- · large font
- · key heading
- · catchy slogan
- · powerful words
- · factual information
- · a specific audience

	Purpose To inform or persuade or both?	Style Formal, friendly, personal, impersonal?	Audience Who is it aimed at?	Organisation Is it structured in a specific way?	Impact How does it make an impact? Any persuasive devices?
Poster 2	Gives information about ...				
Poster 1		The style is ...			

2 Which poster do you find more persuasive? Why?

C 📝 **Add the posters to your reading log. Say which one you prefer and why.**

How did I do?

- Did I identify features of a poster?
- Did I sound persuasive in a role play?
- Did I use a table to compare different posters?
- Did I notice the persuasive devices used to get people interested?

4 and 5 Finding information

A 🅐📖💬🄰🅉 **A poster can be persuasive, informative or both.**

1 What does this map show? Why would it be useful as part of the
Dublin Mountaineer poster?

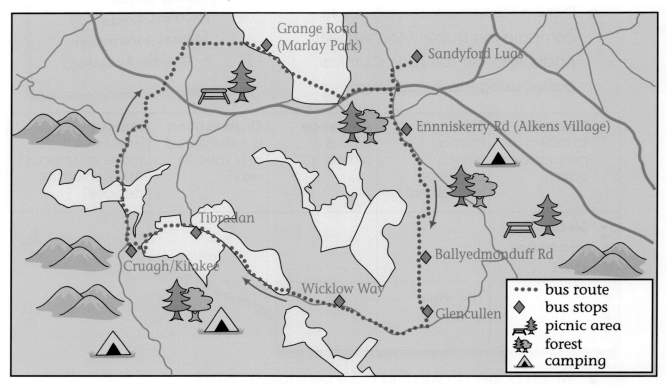

2 Use the map **and** the timetable to answer these questions.

a Where does the bus route start and end?

b Which colour line on the map shows the bus route?

c Does the bus route go clockwise or **anti-clockwise**?

d How many stops does the bus make altogether?

e How long does one complete bus route take?

f How many times does the bus do this trip each day?

g How long does the bus wait between trips?

h In terms of time, which is the shortest stretch of the trip?

3 Ask your partner some questions of your own about the map.

> **Tip**
>
> If you're not
> used to reading
> maps, work with
> a partner.

anti-clockwise *adj., adv.* in the opposite direction
to the movement of the hands of a clock

B  **Prepositions are useful for giving directions.**

Language focus

A **preposition** is a word that comes before a noun to show *how* and *where* things are positioned.

- Prepositions of time tell you *when* something occurred:

  <u>at</u> 11.30 a.m., <u>on</u> Tuesday, <u>by</u> lunch time, <u>since</u> yesterday

- Prepositions of place tell you *where* something occurred:

  <u>at</u> the bus stop, <u>in</u> the bus, <u>under</u> the tree, <u>through</u> the gate

Adverbial phrases that begin with a preposition are sometimes called **prepositional phrases**.

For example: <u>On our walk</u> we climbed a few hills. We followed the path <u>up the mountain.</u>

1 Read these directions for a recommended walk in the area.

  a List all the prepositions and prepositional phrases you can see.

  b What happens if you use an incorrect preposition?

  Example: Follow the path **beyond** Tibradden Mountain.

> From Featherbed, follow the path towards Tibradden Mountain. The path slopes gently up the mountain for 2.5 km to the viewpoint where you can rest and enjoy a wonderful view from the mountain top. Follow the trail down the hill and into the Tibradden Forest until you reach the road. Cross over the road and enter the Cruagh Forest through the gate. Stay on the trail which runs along the river to a popular picnic spot. Walk across a 400 m **bog bridge** and follow the winding path back to Featherbed.

bog bridge *n.* a simple bridge made of planks resting on logs

Tip

Identify the noun or pronoun that comes after each preposition.

2 Complete each sentence with the correct prepositions to describe the bus route on the map. Write them in your notebook.

   a The Dublin Mountaineer heads <u>along</u> … <u>towards</u> …
   b <u>After</u> … it arrives <u>at</u> …
   c It winds its way <u>through</u> … and <u>around</u> …
   d The final trip is <u>between</u> …

> **Any volunteers?**
> Can anyone give directions to different places around your school?

Tip

A sentence can have more than one preposition!

For example: *The bus leaves <u>from</u> Sandyford Luas <u>at</u> 10.00 a.m.*

Did you know?

Prepositions are used in figurative expressions like *"He drove me around the bend"* or *"I'm between a rock and a hard place."* Do you know what these expressions mean? Can you think of some others?

How did I do?

- Did I find information on a map?
- Did I use correct prepositions to give directions?

C 📝 Add the map and timetable to your reading log. How easy or hard was it to find information from them?

6 Talk about films

A 💬 Do you enjoy watching films? With so many to choose from, how do you choose a good one?

1 In groups, discuss some films you've seen.

   a What film have you enjoyed recently?
   b What was it about?
   c Was it based on a book?
   d What did you enjoy about it? What didn't you enjoy?
   e Would you recommend it? What age groups would it appeal to?

2 How do you choose a film to watch?

I like to watch my favourite actors.

I only watch comedies.

My parents decide.

I try to see films that my friends recommend.

I look at the age restriction.

I look at the pictures on the posters.

I read reviews.

3 **a** Which is your favourite **genre**? Tell your group.

b Name some films of different genres that you have seen.

> Fantasy   Science fiction   Adventure   Action   Animal
> Real-life drama   Mystery   Comedy   Suspense

> **genre** *n.* a style with a particular set of characteristics

B 📖 💬 **Identify the genre of a film by looking at the poster or the DVD cover.**

1 From these posters, can you tell which films you would enjoy?

2 Decide what genre each movie is.

3 Film posters give you an idea of what to expect in the film and try to persuade you to watch it. What informative details and persuasive devices can you find in these posters?

4 Order the films on page 125 according to the one you are least keen to watch and the one you are most keen to watch. Give reasons.

*Who can explain the terms **informative** and **persuasive device?***

7 and 8 Analyse film reviews

A **Film reviews give an opinion about a film.**

1 Read the film reviews on page 127. Can you find examples of the following features in both reviews?

A title	personal opinions
basic plot	facts about the film
names of the main characters	a rating
the genre	persuasive language
the age restriction	personal style

2 What other features do the reviews have in common?

B **A review is a personal response. It can be negative or positive.**

Any volunteers? Who can explain the purpose of a film review? Is it to inform a viewer about a film or to persuade the viewer to watch it?

1 Find a sentence in one of the reviews that tells us:
  a the reviewer enjoyed the film very much.
  b the reviewer thinks other people will enjoy the film.

2 Find more powerful synonyms from the reviews to replace the underlined words in these sentences.
  a She is a <u>fine</u> actor.
  b It is a <u>nice</u> story.
  c The message was <u>good</u>.
  d The 3-D images are <u>interesting</u>.
  e The music was <u>enjoyable</u>.

3 Can you find other powerful synonyms in a thesaurus that fit the context of each sentence?

Whale Rider

Rating: ☆☆☆☆
Age restriction: PG 13
Time: 1 hour 45 minutes
Genre: Family drama
Directed by: Niki Caro
Written by: Niki Caro

This is honestly one of the best films I've ever seen! It was shot on location in New Zealand. It is an inspiring story about a young Maori girl's **quest** to win the respect of her grandfather and prove her ability to lead the tribe. I thought the actress who played the role of 'Pai' was brilliant. The film has a positive message about acceptance, **perseverance** and **triumphing** against all odds. It is based on the novel by Maori writer Witi Ihimaera.

I think the age restriction is good because the opening scene might be disturbing for young viewers.

Hugo

Rating: ☆☆☆☆☆
Age restriction: PG
Time: 2 hours 6 minutes
Genre: Mystery and suspense
Directed by:
Martin Scorsese
Written by:
John Logan,
Brian Selznick

Hugo is a touching story about the adventures of a boy who lives in a Paris railway station in 1931. The plot revolves around his quest to unlock a secret his father left him, while keeping out of harm's way! I had enjoyed the book so much (*The Invention of Hugo Cabret* by Brian Selznick) that I wasn't sure I would enjoy the film, but I did! I was totally dazzled by the magical 3-D images and I thought the boy who played Hugo was the perfect actor. The music was lively and suited the story. I highly recommend that you see it.

---

quest *n.* a long search for something that is difficult to find
perseverance *n.* a quality of being steadfast and determined
triumph *n.* to succeed

9 and 10 Present an oral review

> **subjective** *adj.* based on personal beliefs or feelings, rather than based on facts

A 📝 **How much you enjoy a film is subjective. You might love a film that nobody else likes!**

1 Is there a film you've enjoyed recently? Review it.

   a List the basic information about the film. Use key words.

   b Research any information that you might not know.

> Title   Genre   Time   Age restriction   Director   Rating

2 Now write a commentary about different aspects of the film.

> **Setting:** The film was shot on location in New Zealand because that is where the original story came from.
>
> **Characters:** I thought the boy who played Hugo was the perfect actor.
>
> **Plot:** The plot was so exciting and exactly the same as the book.
>
> **Music:** The music went well with the story.

> What was your favourite scene or character? Why? Express your opinion in powerful words.

3 Give the film a rating. You can use stars, faces, a score out of five or even a picture of a glass of water at different levels. Be creative!

B 📝 👥 **Give a speech about your favourite film to try and persuade others to see it too.**

1 Note the key points about your chosen film on a speech card to remind you what to say. Use headings and key words only.

> I think I'll write mine on a clapperboard!

2 Practise your speech with a talk partner. Give each other feedback and try to improve your presentation.

Language focus

Body language is an important part of communication, as well as what you say.

If you stand like this …

… you are communicating that you are shy, scared or not interested.

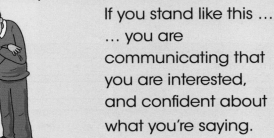

If you stand like this …

… you are communicating that you are interested, and confident about what you're saying.

3 Present your speech with confidence and enthusiasm.

4 Listen to other film reviews presented by your classmates and discuss them in groups. Did the review include important details? Was it persuasive? Can you suggest any ideas to make it sound more appealing?

C 💬 **After your speech, take a vote to see who would like to see the film and who would prefer not to see it.**

How did I do?

- Did I write commentary notes giving my opinion?
- Did I practise and present my oral review with confidence?
- Did I discuss other reviews and offer my own ideas for how to improve them?

D 📝 **Record the film reviews in your reading log. Would you like to read more of them?**

11 and 12 Informal or formal

A 📖 💬 📝 **AZ** **In the past, writing a letter was the only written way to communicate with friends or family living far away.**

1 How do **you** communicate with friends or family who live far away?

Do you ever send letters, post cards or thank you notes?

What's the difference between a friendly letter and a formal one?

When is it appropriate to send a handwritten letter rather than a typed one?

2 Today, emails are a popular form of letter-writing. Discuss this email.

- How would you describe it?
- Who is it to and who is it from?
- What is it about?
- Is the language formal or relaxed?
- Is the language persuasive?

What do the acronyms "RSVP" and "ASAP" stand for?

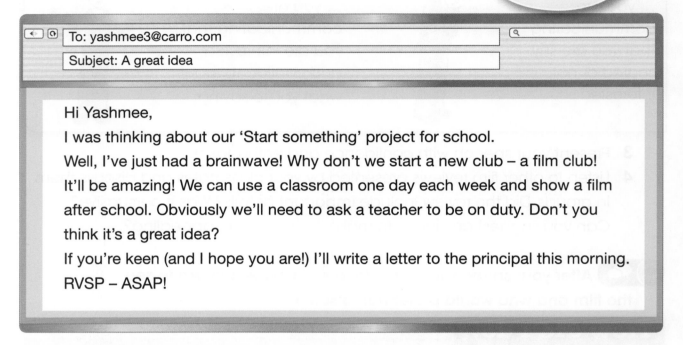

To: yashmee3@carro.com

Subject: A great idea

Hi Yashmee,

I was thinking about our 'Start something' project for school.

Well, I've just had a brainwave! Why don't we start a new club – a film club!

It'll be amazing! We can use a classroom one day each week and show a film after school. Obviously we'll need to ask a teacher to be on duty. Don't you think it's a great idea?

If you're keen (and I hope you are!) I'll write a letter to the principal this morning.

RVSP – ASAP!

Language focus

In informal writing, words are often joined to form **contractions**. When the words are joined, one or more letters are left out. We use an apostrophe to show where these letters were removed.

Example: I will → I'll

Remember, contractions should be avoided in formal writing.

There's something unusual about **won't**. What is it?

3 a Make these words sound less formal by joining them together to make contractions.

> can not   I have   I am   you are   we will   they are

b Write these contractions out in full to sound more formal.

> I'm   you've   you'll   we'd   we're   they've   they'll

1 Who is this letter to? Is it an informal letter or a formal one?

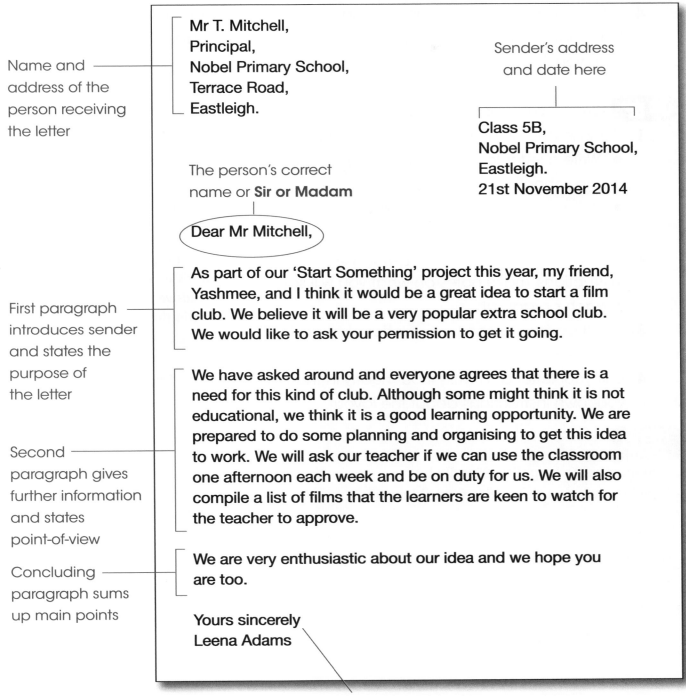

Name and address of the person receiving the letter

Mr T. Mitchell,
Principal,
Nobel Primary School,
Terrace Road,
Eastleigh.

Sender's address and date here

Class 5B,
Nobel Primary School,
Eastleigh.
21st November 2014

The person's correct name or **Sir or Madam**

Dear Mr Mitchell,

First paragraph introduces sender and states the purpose of the letter

As part of our 'Start Something' project this year, my friend, Yashmee, and I think it would be a great idea to start a film club. We believe it will be a very popular extra school club. We would like to ask your permission to get it going.

Second paragraph gives further information and states point-of-view

We have asked around and everyone agrees that there is a need for this kind of club. Although some might think it is not educational, we think it is a good learning opportunity. We are prepared to do some planning and organising to get this idea to work. We will ask our teacher if we can use the classroom one afternoon each week and be on duty for us. We will also compile a list of films that the learners are keen to watch for the teacher to approve.

Concluding paragraph sums up main points

We are very enthusiastic about our idea and we hope you are too.

Yours sincerely
Leena Adams

Yours sincerely if addressed by name
Yours faithfully if addressed to **Sir or Madam**

2 Compare this letter with the email. Think about and discuss the purpose, audience, style and organisation.

3 What persuasive devices can you identify in the text?

4 Write a short set of instructions explaining how to set out a formal letter and what to include in each paragraph. Use the labels to help you.

 Write a persuasive formal letter.

1 Choose one of the topics below or think of an idea of your own.
- Write a letter to your headteacher proposing a new idea for the school.
- Write a letter to your local newspaper asking it to include a children's section.

2 Plan your letter carefully. Following your own instructions, make notes on what you will say in each paragraph.

> I'm sure you'll agree that it's essential to use persuasive language to win them over!

3 Ask a partner to check your letter plan and give you feedback.

4 Edit your letter and write it out neatly in the correct format, following your own instructions about the layout.

Tip

Remember to be polite, friendly but persuasive, and to avoid informal language.

9 Let's perform

Do you enjoy being on the stage? Performing in front of an audience can be fun! You'll begin this unit by performing a well-known nonsense poem. Then you'll use your performance skills and knowledge to stage a play that you've adapted from a story yourself. Finally, you'll have a chance to perform your play to the class!

Vocabulary to learn and use:
stanza, sieve, nonsense, play script, dialogue, performance, sparrow, cast, stage directions, stage properties (props)

1 and 2 Poems to perform

A 📖 💬 **Some poems can be read and enjoyed silently but others are better when read aloud or performed!**

1 Read the first two stanzas of a well-known nonsense poem, on page 134. As you read, clap the beat and enjoy the rhythm.

2 Who are the Jumblies?

3 How many lines are there in each stanza? Which part do you think is the chorus (or refrain)?

4 Discuss any unfamiliar words. Can you work out what they mean? Does it matter if you don't know?

5 For fun, make up your own nonsense verse by changing some of the words, for example: *They went to sea in a …* or *Their heads are … and their hands are …* Try to keep the rhythm and rhyme going.

Did you know?

Edward Lear (1812–88) was an English writer and artist, famous for his nonsense poetry and limericks. He was the 20th child in a family of 21 children!

> Do you know what a sieve is? Can it float? Can you think of any other silly ideas for a boat?

THE JUMBLIES

I. They went to sea in a Sieve, they did,
    In a Sieve they went to sea:
    In spite of all their friends could say,
    On a winter's morn, on a stormy day,
    In a Sieve they went to sea!
    And when the Sieve turned round and round,
    And everyone cried, "You'll all be drowned!"
    They cried aloud, "Our Sieve ain't big,
    But we don't care a button, we don't care a fig!
    In a Sieve we'll go to sea!"
    Far and few, far and few,
    Are the lands where the Jumblies live;
    Their heads are green, and their hands are blue,
    And they went to sea in a Sieve.

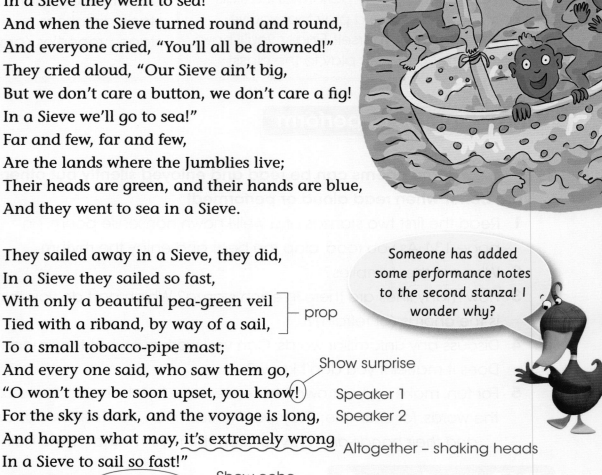

Someone has added some performance notes to the second stanza! I wonder why?

Group 1

II. They sailed away in a Sieve, they did,
    In a Sieve they sailed so fast,
    With only a beautiful pea-green veil
    Tied with a riband, by way of a sail, ⟩ prop
    To a small tobacco-pipe mast;

Group 2

    And every one said, who saw them go,   Show surprise
    "O won't they be soon upset, you know!)   Speaker 1
    For the sky is dark, and the voyage is long,   Speaker 2
    And happen what may, it's extremely wrong
                                            Altogether – shaking heads
    In a Sieve to sail so fast!"

altogether

    Far and few, far and few, — Show echo
    Are the lands where the Jumblies live;   actions
    Their heads are green, and their hands are blue,
    And they went to sea in a Sieve. — All waving

Edward Lear

B 📖 👥 📝 **Performing on stage in front of everyone can be daunting so performing poetry is a good place to start. This poem is fun to perform because there are so many ways you can do it.**

1 Get into small groups and plan your performance.

   a Read the second stanza of the poem and get some ideas from the performance notes that have been added.

   b Discuss ideas for how to perform this poem and use these points to make your own notes.

- Who will say what? You can have more than one narrator and more than one person speaking at a time. Experiment!
- What kind of expression will you use?
- Where will you sit or stand?
- What actions and props will you use?

> **daunting** *adj.*
> overwhelming or scary

2 Practise your performance until everyone knows what to say and do.

3 Take turns to perform the poem to the class or to a younger audience.

Tip

Face the audience so they can see your facial expressions and hear you clearly.

If you learn the poem by heart, you can just focus on your performance.

C 📝 **Add *The Jumblies* to your reading log and rate it.**

> **Any volunteers?**
> Who can say their lines by heart?

How did I do?

- Did I work well in a group to perform the poem?
- Did I remember my part?
- Did I use expression and actions to bring my part to life?

A 💬 **Now that you've performed a poem, get ready to write and perform a play!**

1 Have you read any stories that you've also seen as a film or a play?
2 Listen to your teacher read the beginning of this story about a sparrow. The story comes from Iran and is a modern retelling of an old folk tale.

The Sparrow's Quest

I've read and watched the story of *The Ugly Duckling!*

A hungry sparrow, one cold winter's day, fluttered about hunting for something to eat. At last she saw a movement on an icy pond.

Aha! She thought. A **grub**! And down she swooped, hoping for a meal.
But there was no grub, only a twig blowing in the breeze.
The ice was so cold that the sparrow's feet began to sting.
"Oh, cruel ice!" she exclaimed. "Nothing has ever hurt me as much as this. There's no-one else like you, who can give a poor little bird such pain. How does it feel to be the greatest power there is?"

The ice creaked and cracked as a laugh shivered along his bright surface.
"Powerful? Me?" he growled. "How wrong you are. The sun is much stronger than I am. When the spring comes, he'll shine his hot rays down on me and I'll splinter and melt away. You must ask the sun how it feels to be powerful, little bird."

Retold by *Elizabeth Laird*

> **grub** *n.* the larva of an insect, the word is often used to describe insects or worms

3 What might happen next? What other characters do you think might appear?
4 Do you think this story could be performed? Why?

B 📖 💬 **When a story is adapted into a play, the structure must change.**

1 Read the first part of the story, this time written in the form of a play.

> **Any volunteers?**
> Who can explain how a play script is set out?

An act is a main part of a play. A play can have one or more acts. Each act can have one or more scenes.

A one-act play

The Sparrow's Quest

The title – may give clues about what the play is about

Cast	**Stage props**
Sparrow	Coloured costumes e.g. green for grass
Ice	Masks for the sparrow, sun and worm
Sun	Large, cardboard clouds
The clouds (2–5)	Dry leaves
Wind (2–3)	
The mountain	
The grass (3–5)	
Worm	

Cast list – who the characters are

The number of actors that can play this part

Props – items to be used on stage

Scene – a part of an act of a play

Setting – describes the arrangement of props and characters to show the time and place of the scene

ACT 1, SCENE 1:

Winter. A white sheet, centre stage, represents the frozen ground. A backdrop of clouds and a mountain range, with grass in the foreground. A small sparrow enters looking for a grub to eat.

Stage directions – tell the actor how to behave and speak

SPARROW: (*stamping feet on the ice*) Oh, cold, cruel ice! My feet are in such pain. Nothing could ever hurt me more than you do. How does it feel to be the greatest power there is?

Dialogue – the words the actors say to tell the story

ICE: (*dressed in white, lying on the white sheet, bellows out*) Me? The most powerful? Ha, ha, ha! How wrong you are! When spring comes the sun will shine and I will melt away. Go and speak to the great sun in the sky, little bird.

Enter the sun dressed in yellow with a sun mask. Ice exits the stage, removing the sheet.

SPARROW: (*shielding her face from Sun's rays*) Great sun! Are you the greatest power there is?

SUN: (*proudly*) The greatest power? How can I be, since clouds can cover me and hide me from everyone?

Rewritten play script based on the words of *The Sparrow's Quest* by Elizabeth Laird

Enter Clouds, they move in and cover Sun.

2 Why is it important to have the cast and props listed right at the beginning of the play script?

3 Re-read and discuss the stage directions.

    a What is their purpose?

    b Why are they written in brackets?

    c Would the play script make sense without them?

    d What tense are the stage directions written in? Why?

    e How do the stage directions convey the writer's point-of-view about the story and the characters?

C **Record the story and play script of *The Sparrow's Quest* in your reading log. Would you like to know what happens next?**

4 Creating characters

A **The dialogue, stage directions and props help to create and develop the characters.**

1 Explain what this means in your own words.

2 Read the next part of the play script.

> *Wind breezes in, dressed in long, flowing pieces of cloth, looking mischievous and spins Sparrow around.*
>
> SPARROW: (*spinning around and laughing*) Stop, Wind! Is it true that you are the greatest power there is?
>
> WIND: (*tossing dry leaves playfully into the air*) Little sparrow, how can that be? There is something I can never move, however hard I blow. The mountain is far more powerful than I am. Now catch me if you can!

    a How is the wind's appearance described?

    b What are we told about the wind's personality?

    c Which details describe his behaviour?

    d How does Sparrow react? What does this tell us?

3 How might each character be dressed as part of their characterisation?

Tip

The props list might help you.

The secret is to keep the props and costumes simple but *effective*!

B 📖 📝 **AZ** **Use adjectives to describe the characters in the play so far.**

1 a Choose one adjective from this list for each character.

> cruel   playful   proud   inquisitive

b Use a thesaurus to find synonyms for these adjectives.

Example: strong – mighty – powerful – sturdy

c Order the synonyms from least intense in meaning to most intense.

Example: sturdy, powerful, mighty

Tip

Use a thesaurus. Check that your synonyms fit the context of the character.

Language focus

To form degrees of comparison, sometimes we add the suffixes **er** and **est** to the adjective and sometimes we add *more* or *most*.
Can you work out a rule for when we use each form?
Clue: think about the number of syllables in the adjective.

2 Write these adjectives as degrees of comparison.
Example: mighty, mightier, mightiest

> playful   proud   great   powerful   high

5 Write a play script

(A) 📝 💬 **A play script is like direct speech without any linking narrative.**

1 Practise changing the sentences below into play script form.
   Add stage directions in the present tense.

   Example: "Please can I have some more?" asked the child, quietly.

   > Child: (asking in a quiet voice) Please can I have some more?

   a Sunita replied anxiously, "I don't know the answer."

   b "Please help me!" Tim called out desperately.

   c "You are so funny!" Johanna remarked with an unkind laugh.

   d The spectators clapped and shouted, "Well done, team!"

2 With your talk partner, work out the missing dialogue in the script.
   Write it out correctly into your notebook.

SPARROW: (speaking to the clouds) ...

THE CLOUDS: (being chased away by the wind) ...

SPARROW: (spinning around and laughing) Stop, Wind! Is it true that you are the greatest power there is?

WIND: (tossing some dry leaves into the air) Little sparrow, how can that be? There is something I can never move, however hard I blow. The mountain is far more powerful than I am.

SPARROW: (addressing the mountain) ...

MOUNTAIN: (in a deep, booming voice, pointing to the grass) ...

SPARROW: (speaking wearily to the grass) ...

GRASS: (pointing to the worms beneath the ground) ...

---

3 Swap with another pair and check each other's work. Enjoy reading different versions and give helpful feedback where necessary.

> To make your dialogue unique, why not add another character? What sort of character would fit in?

B 📖 💬 📝 **Plays usually have a climax and a resolution just like any other story.**

> Did it end the way you expected or was it a surprise?

1 Read how this story ends.

The sparrow, who was very tired by now, and faint with hunger, looked around until she saw a worm hole. She stood above it and called down, "Worm, are you there? The grass tells me how powerful you are, the most powerful thing on earth. Tell me, is it true?"

The humble worm had never been asked such a question before. Unwisely, he poked his head out of his hole, and sighed, "Oh, how I wish I was! Then I would never be afraid of being eaten by a hungry sparrow."

Too late, he saw who it was who had called down to him, for at that moment the sparrow opened her beak and began to gobble him up.

Just before he disappeared altogether, the worm managed to gasp, "How does it feel then, cruel sparrow, to be the greatest thing on earth?"

The sparrow swallowed, and wiped her beak on the grass.

"A little less hungry," she said.

Retold by *Elizabeth Laird*

2 Describe the play's plot in three sentences using these starters:

1 A sparrow wanted to know …	2 To find the answer she asked …	3 In the end she realised that …

What does it all mean?

Most stories and plays can be read and understood on different levels.

- the basic story or plot
- a deeper meaning or message
- each person's personal point-of-view, based on their own experiences.

Although *The Sparrow's Quest* has a simple plot, there is a deeper theme or message about the **cyclical** nature of power.

Thinking of your own experience of life, do you think the message of the story is correct? What's your point-of-view?

> **cyclical** *adj.* a group of events that happen in a particular order, one following the other, and that are often repeated

3 With a partner, write the final part of the play script.

- Remember to use a play script format like the one on page 137.
- Include stage directions in brackets.
- Write the dialogue in your own words.

4 Check your work carefully for errors. Ask a partner to proofread it for you and then make your corrections.

6 Perform a play

A 👥 **AZ** **Plays are written to be performed!**

1 In groups, choose one play to perform in front of the class.

- Decide who will play the different parts.
- Decide what props and costumes to use. Keep it simple.
- Practise so you know where to enter, exit and stand.
- Learn your words and actions.
- Don't turn your back on the audience.

Remember to use expressions and body language that suit your character and speak loudly and clearly for everyone to hear!

How did I do?

- Did I set my play out in the correct format?
- Did I use the dialogue and stage directions to describe the characters?
- Did I work well in my group to perform the play?

Term 1 Spelling activities

(A) AZ Compound adjectives

Compound adjectives are formed by joining two or more words together with a hyphen: *light + hearted = light-hearted*

1 Use words from the box to form compound adjectives of your own.

> down prepared well fun go fashioned hearted
> non loving made happy earth known up date
> fiction man to old kind behaved lucky

2 Draw pictures to show the difference in meaning between these sentences:
   I saw a man eating crocodile.   *I saw a man-eating crocodile.*

3 What parts of speech make up these words? lift-off, fighter-pilot

4 Use each one in a sentence to a partner.

5 Some compound words have become one word without a hyphen. Separate these examples into their component words and identify the parts of speech.
   Example: blackboard: → black + board   (adjective + noun)

> armchair dragonfly shipwreck website background
> highlight without football grandmother pancake inside

(B) AZ ant or ent?

There are no rules to help you decide if a word ends in **ant** or **ent**, just some helpful hints.

● If **ment** has been added to a verb to form a noun, it is always **ent.**

● If the root word ends in **soft c** or **g**, use **ent**. If it ends in **hard c** or **g**, use **ant.**

1 Say the nouns that are formed by adding **ment** to these verbs:
   Example: develop + ment → development

> govern engage agree manage arrange improve enjoy

2 Work out whether to use **ant** or **ent** for these words:

> intellig[ant/ent]   magnific[ent/ant]   dilig[ent/ant]   extravag[ent/ant]
> applic[ent/ant]   eleg[ent/ant]   rec[ent/ant]   signific[ent/ant]
> transluc[ent/ant]   urg[ent/ant]   deterg[ent/ant]

C AZ Use that root

1 a Identify the **word root** of these words: mystify, mystic, mystical, mystique.
  b Check you understand them all and discuss how their meanings are related.
2 Add a prefix to create a verb meaning the opposite of **mystify**.
3 Find an adjective, an adverb and a noun related to **mystery**.
4 What is the root of these words and what does it mean?

> graphite autograph calligraphy geography graphic bibliography photograph

5 **Graffiti** comes from the same word root. How is its meaning related?
6 How can knowing the root help you spell or understand related words?

D AZ Doubling consonants

Some words double the final consonant when you add **ed** or **ing**.
If the word ends in:

1 vowel + **l, d, n, g**, or **t**	double the final consonant	trav**el** → trave**lled** n**ag** → na**gg**ing
2 vowels + a consonant	**don't** double the final consonant	w**ait** → waited sl**eep** → slee**p**ing

1 Discuss which words double the final consonant with **ed** or **ing**:

> cool   fulfil   wait   equal   beg   croon   shun   drool   admit   refer
> bleed   lead   pin   creak   speed   spot   read   float   bat

2 Use these words to help you write a rule for spelling adverbs formed from adjectives ending in **ful**, e.g. helpful → helpfully.

> thankful   awfully   dreadful   fearfully   painful

E AZ Plurals

Some nouns do not change in the plural form, for example one haiku, many haiku.

1 Use these nouns in sentences in both the singular and plural:
  fish, trout, sheep, aircraft, deer, species, salmon

Term 2 Spelling activities

A AZ More plural rules

When nouns end in **f** or **fe**, change the **f** or **fe** to **v** before adding **s** or **es**. half → halves

Tip

Some words can be spelled either way. What about *Snow White and the Seven Dwar … ?*

1 a Write the plurals of these words: **self, knife, wife, yourself, penknife, housewife**.

   b Are the plurals of compound words ending in **f** or **fe** formed any differently?

   c Find the plurals of these words: **roof, cliff, chief, handkerchief, safe, chef, giraffe** (clue: they are exceptions!).

B AZ Word origins – Days of the week

1 Can you work out which day of the week was named after each of these important sky objects and ancient gods? The day names have changed over time, but you can still see the origins.

> Saturn – the Roman god of sowing or seeds
>
> Woden (Odin) – the most powerful Norse god, the Moon
>
> Thor – the Norse god of thunder

C AZ Use prefixes to form antonyms

A prefix is a group of letters added to the front of a root word to change its meaning. Some prefixes form antonyms (words of opposite meaning).

2 Try adding these prefixes to the words below to make antonyms. Say them out loud to check which one sounds right.

> dis   un   in   im   ir   il

> satisfied   legible   polite   credible   regular   formal
> formal   rational   probable   conscious   legal   visible

Check with a dictionary if you get stuck.

3 Write a pair of sentences for six of the words and their antonyms, using each prefix only once.

4 Find at least two more words with each prefix and work out their root antonyms.

D AZ Explore opposites

Opposites can be created by adding prefixes and suffixes, or the opposite can be a completely different word.

1 Talk about how these opposites have been created:

> day – night   salted – unsalted   useful – useless   valuable – worthless
> fiction – non-fiction   subtract – add   early – late   do – redo

2 Discuss the opposite of 'light'. What do you notice?

E AZ Comparative spelling

1 Revise how to form comparative adjectives.

> small → smaller → smallest   intelligent → more intelligent → most intelligent

   a How are the different methods formed?
   b When would you use each?
2 Identify the spelling rule for these comparatives:
   a large, larger, largest; rude, ruder, rudest; brave, braver, bravest
   b funny, funnier, funniest; silly, sillier, silliest; bossy, bossier, bossiest
   c hot, hotter, hottest; big, bigger, biggest; sad, sadder, saddest
   d Explain why these words do not follow the pattern in (c): cool, cooler, coolest; sharp, sharper, sharpest; great, greater, greatest.

F AZ Spelling patterns

1 Group these words according to their vowel sounds and write the vowel sound as a heading for each group.

> moon   claw   bride   through   dry   fort   shore   write
> caught   route   sort   suit   flute   high   shoot   lied

2 a Say these words: circle, grace, receive, cereal, city, cycle. What sound does the c make?
   b Which letters follow c in these words?
   c Write down and say two words with each letter combination: **cl, cr, ca, cu**.
   d How does c sound when it is followed by **l, r, a** or **u**?
3 a Sort these words according to the sound **g** makes: garden, gym, gel, grate, glass, giraffe, gum.
   b Why are these words exceptions: gift, begin, give, girl, get?
   c Discuss how you can use the spelling to help you pronounce some words.

Term 3 Spelling activities

(A) AZ Unusual plurals

Some words have unusual plurals especially if they come from other languages.
Synopsis comes from Ancient Greek. Its plural form is **synopses**.

1 Check the meanings of these words that also come from Ancient Greek, and write a sentence using the plural form for three of them.

> ellipsis   emphasis   hypnosis   analysis   crisis   oasis

2 **Phenomenon** also comes from Ancient Greek. Find out its plural form.

3 **Criteria** is a plural word. What is its singular form?

(B) AZ More word roots

1 Find the root word for each of these job names: mountaineer, teacher, artist, engineer, charioteer, archaeologist, auctioneer.

2 **Sign** comes from the French word *signe*, which came from the Latin *signum*.
   a Look up the different meanings of *sign* and write a sentence for each meaning.
   b Think up words related to *sign*, for example **resign, signal**.
   c Use each word in a sentence to show its meaning.

3 How does your knowledge of the word origin help you spell related words?

(C) AZ Noun or verb?

Some words can be a noun or a verb depending on the context. They are spelled the same but pronounced differently.

In words with two syllables, the stress is usually on the first syllable for a noun (PREsent) and on the second for a verb (preSENT).

1 Practise pronouncing each of these words first as a noun and then as a verb.

> project   insult   object   produce   contest   rebel

2 Use each word as a *noun* and then as a *verb* in sentences, showing the stressed syllable in CAPITAL LETTERS.

D AZ More spelling rules for the suffix –ing

1 Discuss the rule for forming these present participles:

> smile → smiling, freeze → freezing, shine → shining

2 Discuss the rule for forming these present participles: try → trying, cry → crying.

3 Using all the rules you have learned, write the present participle of each verb.

> sleep   think   leave   fly   sit   eat   grind   destroy
> dig   kneel   strive   spy   choose   win   dismay

4 What are the present participles for know, draw, glow, stew? What new rule can you write for these words?

Tip

You have already learned some rules for adding –**ing** in the Term 1 Spelling activities.

E AZ Choose the right synonym

It is important to look at the context of the word when you choose a synonym. Not every synonym is right in a particular context.

1 Check the meaning of these synonyms and write a sentence to show how each one should be used:
   - carnival
   - festival
   - function
   - event.

2 Words with a similar meaning can also differ in intensity. Order these words from the least to the most intense.
   a We had a wonderful/great/amazing day at the carnival.
   b The puppet show was amusing/hilarious/funny.
   c The food was delicious/edible/heavenly.

F AZ i before e

1 Find a word containing *ie* or *ei* to fit these meanings:
   a someone who steals something
   b to mislead someone
   c a portion of something
   d short – taking little time
   e the top of a room
   f a brother's or sister's daughter.

Tip

Put **i** before **e** except after **c** if the sound is **ee**.
When the sound is not **ee**, use **ei**.
When the **c** makes the sound **sh**, use **ie**.
Exceptions: *seize, weird, friend, mischief.*

Toolkit

There are eight formal parts of speech.

Parts of speech

Nouns	Pronouns
Naming words for people, places and things Proper nouns – names of people and places Common nouns – names of things Abstract nouns – names of feelings and ideas that we can't see, hear or touch Collective nouns – names of groups of things	• stand in for nouns to stop repetition • show possession *mine, yours, his, hers, its, ours, theirs*
Prepositions	**Verbs**
A word or group of words used directly before a noun or pronoun to show place, direction, time	Describe action, a state of being or having something **Tense** Different forms of a verb to show whether an action takes place in the past, present or future
Interjections	**Conjunctions**
Words added to a sentence to convey emotion *Ouch! Oh no! Ah!*	Connectives that link words, groups of words, sentences or paragraphs
Adverbs	**Adjectives**
Describe or give more information about a verb, adjective, phrase, or other adverb **Adverbials** Groups of words (phrases and clauses) that act as adverbs	Describe nouns to tell you more about them Groups of words (adjectival phrases and clauses) can also act as adjectives

Review, edit and revise

Not all writing needs all of these features. Think about your purpose and assess what you have used. Can you do better?

	What did I check for?
1	I followed the instructions for the activity.
2	I checked my spellings using a dictionary.
3	I read my work through for sense and flow.
4	I used a variety of sentences.
5	My sentences start in different ways.
6	My sentences make sense and are interesting and purposeful.
7	I used the correct punctuation (. , ; : ? ! " " ')
8	I did not repeat the same words and phrases.
9	I chose my words carefully, considering my purpose and my audience.
10	I replaced common words and phrases with more interesting ones.
11	I used a variety of descriptive words and phrases – adjectives, verbs, adverbs.
12	My sentences flow well and make sense.
13	I used simple sentences.
14	I used compound sentences.
15	I used complex sentences with different structures: • adverbials to start sentences, in the middle and at the end • subordinating connectives for different purposes (showing time, manner and place) • long and short forms of tenses
16	I used tenses consistently in narrative and dialogue.
17	I used first/third person narrative consistently.
18	I used topic sentences paragraphs, headings or chapters to organise my work.

Golden rules of speech making

1 Make cue cards using key words only.

6 Don't fidget or make distracting body movements.

2 Practise your speech well so that you are not nervous.

7 Use appropriate expression.

3 Know what you want to say well enough, so that you do not have to read out your notes.

8 Be enthusiastic.

9 End strongly.

4 Keep eye contact with your audience.

10 Be ready to answer questions.

5 Speak clearly and loudly, so that everyone can hear you.

The writing process

Good writing doesn't just happen – you have to practise and follow a process.

Step 1: Plan

Purpose	What is its aim?	Entertain, inform, instruct, explain, persuade?
Audience	Who will read it?	Adults, children, teenagers, friends, unknown people?
Language	How formal should it be?	Formal or informal? Include slang, jargon, colloquial/idiomatic language, figurative and literal language?
Layout	How will it be organised?	What format will it have (letter, story, report, etc.)? Will it have headings, paragraphs, chapters, sections?

Step 2: Write

Write your first draft without stopping or getting distracted. Focus on good, creative, original ideas.

- Follow the right structure and layout: story, summary, dialogue, explanation, etc.
- Use language and vocabulary to fit the style, e.g. narrative person, tense, formal/informal
- Include details to bring your writing to life.

Step 3: Edit

Check and improve your writing.

- **Check:** Read your work. Does it make sense? Is the main idea clear? Has anything been left out? Can anything unnecessary be taken out?
- **Ask for feedback:** Can someone else spot any problems you've missed?
- **Improve:** Revise your language and vocabulary. Use strong verbs, descriptions and comparisons.
- **Correct:** Fix errors in your grammar, spelling and punctuation. Does each sentence start with a capital letter and end with a full stop, question mark or exclamation mark? Are the tenses and prepositions correct? Spellings?

Step 4: Present

Complete your final version with as few mistakes as possible:

- Re-read to check for flow and final errors (use a spell check).
- Write it out neatly in joined-up handwriting or type it out using IT.
- Illustrate or display your work creatively.
- Be ready to explain and talk about your writing to others.

Reading strategies

Don't forget to read for pleasure too!

What you want to do	Skill to use	How to do it
Get the main idea	skim	Read the text quickly to get the general idea. Focus on key words relevant to your task.
Locate specific information	Scan	Run your eyes quickly along the lines looking for specific key words.
Understand unfamiliar words	Read in context	Read sentences before and after the word to help work out its meaning. Use your general knowledge to help you. Use a dictionary only after analysing the word in context.
Work out what's going to happen	Predict	Use the title and illustrations to find clues on what the text will say. Study the format and layout for further clues as to the type of text you are reading.
Understand the text as a whole	Read closely	Use your predictions before you read to help you read everything carefully, concentrating on the details. Read once more to check your understanding.
Write or say main points	Summarise	Skim paragraphs for the main idea. Explain the main idea of each paragraph in a few words of your own.
Understand what you see	Use visual literacy	Notice important details to unlock meaning: • colours, labels, captions and other text • visual conventions, e.g. in cartoons • facial expressions, gestures and movements.
Use what you know to understand the text	Use prior knowledge	What you already know can help you to: • understand a character's feelings • imagine a setting • understand why things happen • see how the information is useful • connect information in new ways.
Explore a text in detail to understand its deeper meaning	analyse	Search for underlying meaning, evidence, comparisons and contrasts in the way text is organised and in what is said to help you form your own opinions and assess the content.

Researching information

Sources of information

1

library	journals
text books	tweets
encyclopaedias	blogs
dictionary and	interviews
thesaurus	leaflets
websites (intranet	posters
or internet)	timetables
newspapers	official reports
magazines	television
diaries	

2 Where would you look to find these different kinds of information?
- more interesting words
- information for a project
- what is going on in the world now
- all about another country, city or place
- family or local history
- what other people think about a topic
- how to do or make something

3 Read your work aloud to check for sense and flow.
- Do all your sentences make sense?
- Are any words wrong?
- Have any words been missed out?
- Are any sentences too long to read easily?
- Have you linked ideas and sentences using connectives?
- Are you writing narrative or dialogue? Have you used the correct verb tenses?

4 Is your punctuation accurate?

5 Have you used capital letters for all the proper nouns?

6 Make all your changes and read through one last time.

Online research

Pros and cons

Lots of information available

Any topic you can think of

More information than you'll ever need

Very convenient

Easy-to-use and to find information

Can become the only source of information

Other sources are neglected

Little thinking involved

Danger of copying - plagiarism

Too much information

Inappropriate material available

To some, this resource is unavailable

How do you take notes on the information you've found?

1 Skim the information to check it is what you need.
2 Scan the information for relevant words and details.
3 Jot down headings, key words and phrases on a mind map.
4 Summarise the information in your own words.

Writing instructions

1 Put your instructions in order.
2 Number the instructions with words or numbers: (1, 2, 3 …, first, second, third …)
3 Use command verbs for the main instruction (use, place, cut, write …)
4 Check the instructions by making sure you could follow them.

> 1. Measure   2. Cut   3. Stick

Ordering your thoughts

To order an argument, you might use the following words:

> 1. firstly, to begin with, start
>
> 2. secondly, then, next
>
> 3. thirdly, finally, in conclusion

Poet's corner

It really helps to know the jargon. You have learnt some of this before but we've included new information too!

When we speak **literally**, we mean exactly what we say. When we speak figuratively, we use words imaginatively to create unusual images.

Figures of speech:

Similes compare one thing to another using the words *like* or *as*. We often use them in colloquial or everyday language: *as warm as toast, as quick as lightning, like two peas in a pod.*

Metaphors compare one thing to another without using *like* or *as*. *She has a heart of gold. He is an angel.*

Personification is a type of metaphor where an object or thing is given human characteristics.

The sun glares furiously across the horizon. Shop doorways keep their mouths shut.

Sound effects: the sound words make is often very important in poetry – as important as the meaning.

- **Alliteration** is when a consonant sound is repeated at the beginning of several words for effect. *Peter Piper picked a peck of pickled pepper. Six snakes slithered stealthily.*

- **Assonance** is when vowel sounds are repeated. It is often used for internal rhymes. *The moon will soon rise over the dune.*

- **Onomatopoeia** uses words that include sounds similar to the noises being described.

The driver honked the horn. The kitten meowed piteously.

- **Repetition** repeats words, phrases, sounds or stanzas to create echoes or other special effects.

  Rhyme appears in the middle or end of lines (often in a pattern ABCB). They can be full or half rhymes.

- **Full rhyme:** the end sounds correspond exactly – *flight, sight, white,* etc.

- **Half rhyme:** the final sounds are similar – *bold/bald, feel/spill, body/lady*

- **Internal rhyme:** two or more words in a line have a full or half rhyme – *I am the <u>daughter</u> of Earth and <u>Water</u>.*

Rhythm is a sound pattern (a beat) that comes from the repetition of stressed and unstressed syllables – the way we say the words. Some poems have a set number of syllables or beats per line.

Mood is created in poetry by the sounds of words as well as the images and meaning they create. Long, soft vowel sounds help create a mysterious mood; short harder consonant sounds create energy and urgency.

Narrative poems tell a story – they follow story conventions but they don't have to follow the same grammatical rules as narrative text.

Synopsis of Cinderella

Cinderella lives happily until her mother dies. Her new stepmother and two stepsisters take every opportunity to be cruel to Cinderella, and when her father dies, they banish her to the kitchen to act as their servant. One day, the King invites all unmarried girls to a ball at the palace, for his son, the Prince, to choose a bride.

Cinderella cannot go as she has only her ragged clothes to wear. Suddenly, her fairy godmother appears and magically changes a pumpkin into a coach, mice into horses and Cinderella's rags into a beautiful gown and shoes, but she warns Cinderella to return home before the stroke of midnight.

Cinderella dances all night with the Prince. As she hears the clock strike midnight, she flees, leaving behind one tiny glass slipper. The prince searches everywhere for the owner of the slipper. Cinderella's stepmother and stepsisters try in vain to squeeze their feet into the shoe, but it fits Cinderella perfectly. She and the Prince marry and live happily ever after.

Space biography fact files

Neil Armstrong (1930–2012)

Neil Armstrong was an American astronaut and the first person to walk on the Moon in July 1969, along with Buzz Aldrin, who was the second person to walk on the Moon.

Armstrong was born in Ohio and from the age of two he developed a love for flying. In high school, he took flying lessons and had his student flight certificate before his driving licence! He was also an active Boy Scout. After school, he studied aeronautical engineering and later became a naval aviator and test pilot. He made his first space flight in 1966.

After his final space mission, he became a university professor.

Liu Yang (1978–   )

Liu Yang began training as an astronaut in 2010. In June 2012, she became China's first female astronaut to go into space. She went with two other crew members on a 13-day mission to China's space station, Tiangong 1. This was the first time China had sent crew to the station and the mission was part of their preparations for a permanent space station in 2020.

As a cargo pilot, Liu Yang displayed great skill and composure when her jet hit a flock of birds but she was still able to land the damaged aircraft safely.

Liu Yang is a Major in the People's Liberation Army Air Force.

Timothy Peake (1972-   )

Tim Peake is a British astronaut. In 2015 he will become the first British citizen to live and work on the ISS for a long-duration mission of six months.

He was born in the United Kingdom and after school he became an officer, and later a General, in the British Army. He is also a test pilot and a helicopter flying instructor.

As part of his training, he has had to live underground in isolation for a week and has spent 12 days in an underwater base 20 m under the sea.

Peake enjoys skiing, scuba diving, cross-country running and reading.

Acknowledgements

The authors and publishers acknowledge the following sources of copyright material and are grateful for the permissions granted. While every effort has been made, it has not always been possible to identify the sources of all the material used, or to trace all copyright holders. If any omissions are brought to our notice, we will be happy to include the appropriate acknowledgements on reprinting.

p. 22 'Three fishes: a tale from India' is retold by Heather Forest, reprinted from www.storyarts.org; p. 40 adapted from blog entry by Sunita Williams, NASA; p. 47 'A bitter morning' haiku from *The Zen Haiku and Other Zen Poems* (1983) by James Hackett, by permission of the author; p. 47 'Swifts' haiku by Chris Jones from http://callandresponsehaiku.wordpress.com/ haiku-archive (Longbarrow Press); p. 51 'Listen' by Telcine Turner, used with permission p. 52 'Wind' by Dionne Brand. Material from *Earth Magic* written by Dionne Brand and illustrated by Eugine Fernandes is used by permission of Kids Cans Press Ltd., Toronto. Text © 1979, 2006 Dionne Brand; p. 55 from *Welcome to Olympus* by Jenny Koralek, © Jenny Koralek 1988, published by Cambridge University Press, reproduced with permission; p. 60 from 'The Cat Who Came Indoors', retold by Hugh Tracey from *NELSON MANDELA'S FAVOURITE AFRICAN FOLKTALES* edited by Nelson Mandela. Copyright © 2002 in this selection by Tafelberg Publishers Ltd. Used by permission of W.W. Norton & Company, Inc and Tafelberg Publishers; p. 64 excerpt from 'The Grendel' from *Myths and Legends* by Anthony Horowitz, Kingfisher Books, © Anthony Horowitz, 1985; p. 92 'Lord Neptune' © Judith Nicholls 1990, from *DRAGONSFIRE* by Judith Nicholls, published by Faber & Faber. Reprinted by permission of the author; p. 93 'The Shell' by Vilma Dubé, used with kind permission of the author; p. 95 'At the End of a School Day' by Wes Magee, used by permission of the author; p. 109 from *The Iron Man* by Ted Hughes, published by Faber and Faber Limited; p. 113 'Nine Questions for a Princess' from *The Magic Drum and Other Favourite Stories*, by Sudha Murty, Puffin India; p. 120-123 map and timetable adapted and used with permission of the Dublin Mountaineer Partnership; p. 136 excerpts from 'The Sparrow's Quest' in *Pea Boy and Other Tales from Iran* retold by Elizabeth Laird, Frances Lincoln, 2009, used by permission of the publisher;

Cover artwork: Bill Bolton

The publisher is grateful to the following expert reviewers: Samina Asif, Lois Hopkins, Mary Millet, Lynne Ransford.

Photographs

p10 top l-r © Andrey_Kuzmin / iStock, © GlobalP / iStock, © amattel / iStock, © GlobalP / iStock, bottom l-r © GlobalP / iStock, © GlobalP / iStock, © JackF / iStock, © GlobalP / iStock; p24 t-b © North Wind Picture Archives / Alamy, © Everett Collection Historical / Alamy, © adoc-photos/Corbis, © Image Asset Management Ltd. / Alamy, © Bettmann/CORBIS; p25 t-b © The Art Gallery Collection / Alamy, © Time & Life Pictures/Getty Images, © Picture Press / Alamy, © ITAR-TASS Photo Agency / Alamy, © RIA Novosti / Alamy, © NG Images / Alamy, Courtesy of NASA; p29 t © AFP/Getty Images, b © pedrosala / iStock / Thinkstock; p30 © RIA Novosti / Alamy; p36 t Courtesy of NASA; c © Jupiterimages / Stockbyte / Thinkstock. b © Cathy Yeulet / Hemera / Thinkstock; p38 tl © SerrNovik / iStock / Thinkstock, tr © anyaberkut / iStock / Thinkstock, b Courtesy of NASA; p40 t Courtesy of NASA, b Courtesy of NASA; p45 r © Jewellery specialist / Alamy, l © Phil Cawley / Alamy; p69 © Warner Brothers / AF archive / Alamy; p76 © Tony Lilley / Alamy; p81 t © Carsten Peter/Speleoresearch & Films/National Geographic/Getty Images, b © Carsten Peter/Speleoresearch & Films/National Geographic/Getty Images; p82 © Carsten Peter/Speleoresearch & Films/National Geographic/Getty Images; p84 l © Carsten Peter/Speleoresearch & Films/National Geographic/Getty Images, r © Carsten Peter/Speleoresearch & Films/National Geographic/Getty Images; p85 © Carsten Peter/Speleoresearch & Films/National Geographic/Getty Images; p119 © koosen / iStock / Thinkstock; p125 l-r © Paramount Pictures / AF archive / Alamy, © REX/Snap Stills, © Warner Brothers / AF archive / Alamy

Key: *t* = top, *c* = centre, *b* = bottom, *l* = left, *r* = right.